COCKNEY BOY IN ESSEX

D1391323

COCKNEY BOY IN ESSEX

C. V. SMITH

Egon Publishers Ltd.
19 Baldock Road Letchworth
Herts

First published in 1978

Printed by
S. G. Street & Co. Ltd.
Church Street Baldock
Herts SG7 5AF

ISBN 0 905858 03 4

To those who, when fishes flew and forests walked, shared themselves and their village with a sick child and anchored within his greedy hands the draft of this, their book.

CHAPTER ONE

I remember my Mother telling me that memory is a nursery where children grown old play with broken toys. I do not think that that was hers; she must have borrowed it from someone else. What she knew of philosophy was packed flat between the gilt boards of "East Lynne" and "John Halifax, Gentleman". But, nursery or not, memory is "queer". Just when you are not expecting it it digs into forgotten pockets of the past and highlights something you would have sworn was as dead as the dodo. Shortly before I retired I saw on a plaque commemorating the opening of a one-time workhouse the line: "The poor ye have with you always." And before you could say Llanfairfechan I was back, at the age of seven, to 1904, with eggs at twenty-four a shilling, back, too, to something of my Father's, something he held true as surely as he held true that Mother was the corner-stone of his existence:

"God bless the squire and his relations,
And keep us in our proper stations."

When you were poor in those days you *were* poor, and if you earned thirty shillings a week you paid income tax and your neighbours touched their hats and called you "Sir". It was the era of the pawnshop. Wives "popped" their husbands' suits on Monday and redeemed them on Saturday in time for them to be pressed for church on Sunday. Living was cheap, it is true. You could get a basin of jam from the "oil-shop" for a penny or, for tuppence more, a saveloy, a faggot and a dollop of pease-pudding, all in hot gravy, from the pork-butcher's on the corner. And, believe it or not, a good suite of furniture (fire-irons and fender thrown in) would cost you no more than a modest ten pounds.

It was uncomfortable to be poor, but poverty was no disgrace. And it had its compensations. I can recall going to the Town Hall and coming away with as much soup as I could carry in Mother's biggest jug; and often, before the out-patients were admitted, limping on thin legs to the London Hospital in Whitechapel Road for a bowl of beef dripping. And poverty — for me at least — meant one thing above all: Essex. In the summer of 1904 I went down with bronchitis and double pneumonia. It was serious. The doctor, at sixpence a time, was in and out of the house day and night for a week. Father was working as a platelayer for the Great Eastern Railway, and there was not much money. He pleaded for overtime to earn more but, not getting it, Mother was forced to pawn her wedding-ring and her sewing machine, two of her most cherished possessions. The day came when the doctor told Mother, "The crisis will come tonight. If he survives it he'll be all right; if he doesn't —". It was then that grandmother came. She brought with her a coloured rubber ball and salvation, nursing me and teaching me to walk all over again. Then she whisked me away for the sun and air that were to transform me from a sickly child to one who, over the years, was to blossom to health and strength. I was not so ignorant as to think when I first saw

10

a field of barley that shrimps grew on stalks, but I was next door to such ignorance. The flowers I knew grew in a window box on the kitchen sill and beyond, in the triangular patch of earth showered with black "confetti" whenever the trains thundered past a few feet above my head. There may have been blooms other than marigolds somewhere in the world; if so, I did not know about them.

Thomas Hood begins one of his best-loved poems with the lines:

> "I remember, I remember
> The house where I was born."

I cannot think of one single reason for wanting to remember the house where *I* was born, for the "house" was a miserable block of London flats notorious for communal flights of unwashed steps, gas-jets high on anaemic walls and, on every landing, lavatories that boasted doors only so long as the weather was mild enough for the poorer tenants not to be tempted when others lay abed by the prospect of a week or two's free fuel. There is, however, every reason for wanting to remember the house where I was not born: Scotts Farm, Moreton. It was to Scotts Farm that grandmother rushed me. As that was seventy years ago and as, recently, I returned there on my own two legs, I like to think that grandmother — bless her! — not only got me well but, over many a trying month, made a reasonably good job of me.

There had been an earlier farm (Scotts, alias Embley's) which had stood on the same site. This had been sold in 1729 by the Lord of the Manor for £3,800. The date is interesting. A year later Viscount Charles Townsend, one-time Secretary of State, retired to his home in Norfolk, where he encouraged the growing of turnips and

11

introduced the four-year rotation of crops: roots, barley, clover and wheat. The present Scotts Farm was built some time prior to Tuesday, 20th December, 1887, when it was sold by auction at the "King's Head" inn, Chipping Ongar. The catalogue of the sale described it as "a valuable small Farm containing 34 acres, 3 roods and 2 poles, situated by the roadway in the Parish of Moreton, a short distance from the village, about 3½ miles from Ongar station, and 6 miles from Epping and Harlow. It comprises a newly-erected weather-boarded and slated dwelling-house containing 2 parlours, kitchen, dairy, 4 bedrooms, box-room, a tiled beer-house with oven and 2 coppers, and a capital piece of garden." That — especially the tiled beer-house bit — must have been enough to whet anyone's appetite, but there was more to come: the farm buildings. These included "a barn, a stable for 3 horses with chaff bin, a horse shed with 2 bays, a timber and tiled bullock shed with 5 bays, a cow house with calf pen, a poultry and tool house, and a timber and tiled cart lodge with 3 bays." By this time, I imagine, prospective buyers would have been foaming at the mouth and fingering deep down in their "Sunday best" their precious golden guineas. They were going to need them. The catalogue droned on: "The purchaser will be required to pay for the timber the sum of £24, at which it has been valued, and for the fallows and rent thereon, tillages, wheat, straw and dung at market value (if any) and all things usually taken and paid for by valuation as between out-going and incoming tenants, such valuation to be made by two indifferent persons or their umpires."

There was no indication as to what the tools in or out of the tool-house might have been. That was disappointing. I had hoped to find some reference to the two types of scythes one of grandfather's men had once told me about. There had been the factory ones and the furnace ones.

"I don't 'old wi' they fact'ry 'uns," he had said. "They got a nick in the back where it jines the blade, an' grass an' stuff gits ketched there. Gimme the furnace 'uns. They're all on a piece an' no 'anky-panky. Sides, yer kin 'ang 'em in an apple-tree an' run the rust outta them times yer swallers a pint."

I wondered, too, why the brick oven at the end of the wall fronting the road had not been mentioned for, in it, grandmother baked the best bread in Moreton. She piled it with faggots, lit it and, when it was hot enough, slid in on a wooden peel sad little dollops of dough. There they stayed till the good Lord blessed them and they were "done". What intrigued me most about the oven was what grandmother called the "watch". This was a quartz pebble built into the back which, when the temperature was "ter rights, boy," blazed with the spite of an ogre's eye. Nothing smells better than newly-baked bread and, when I think back to grandmother's, I think back to "Farmer" Cobbett. "Give me," he said, "for a beautiful sight, a neat and smart woman, heating her oven and setting her bread! And if the bustle does make the sign of labour glisten on her brow, where is the man that would not kiss that off, rather than lick the plaster from the cheek of a duchess!"

I have already referred to the first Scotts Farm. I mention it again because I am puzzled. In the "Abstract of the Title of Mr. William Cozens to the Manor of Nether Hall (alias Bouchers Hall) and to several Messuages, Lands and Premises in Moreton," dated 3rd January, 1729, there was this: "It is witnessed that the said Mr. William Cozens, in consideration of the sum of £3,800 paid by Robert Tindall and of 10/0d. paid by John Morgan, did grant, bargain, sell, release and confirm unto the said Robert Tindall and John Morgan all that Farm commonly called or known by the name of Scotts

13

(alias Embleys) or otherwise, with all the Lands, Meadows, Pastures, Fieldings, Outhouses, Buildings and Appurts thereunto belonging or therewith used and enjoyed, situate and being in the Parish of Moreton aforesaid. All the said premises now, or are, or late were in the several tenures or occupations of William Schooling and James Edick, or one of them or one of their under-tenants, together with all and singular the woods, trees, commons, roads and watercourses."

Having regard to the £3,800 paid by Robert Tindall for his enjoyment of "all that Farm" and its "Appurts", I am at a loss to understand why his co-purchaser got away with the insignificant sum of 10/0d. Perhaps the Lord of the Manor suddenly experienced a twinge of conscience. Perhaps he was putting into practice the gentlemanly creed of doing his duty in that state of life into which it had pleased God to call him. Perhaps he was just being kind. I rather incline to this last, for a Register of Rents for 1769 shows that a Mr. King paid to him as quit rent for that year the princely sum of 4d.! (Quit rent was, I believe, a rent payable to the Lord of the Manor by freeholders and copyholders, being an acquittal of all other services.)

It has often been said that a song or a scent has the evocative power of recalling the things of far away and long ago. It needed only the word "bedrooms" to recall one of mine. Somewhere among that catalogued four, when Scotts Farm was sold by auction at the "King's Head", was the one I had later slept in. It was, I recall, lavender-bag-and-Sunday-fresh, with a window peeping down the hill to the church and over the fields to the white skyward-thrust of Moreton Mill. Bedtime was a big adventure. Grandmother knelt with me on the sloping floor while I besought Matthew, Mark, Luke and John not only to bless my bed but to post an angel at each of its corners. Then she slid a warming pan between the sheets, tucked me in and gave me a bundle of old books. "Muse yerself wi' these," she would say, "till I goo an' git yer Eppses." In the morning, on the ladder-back chair by the side of the bed, would be a bar of Fry's "Five Boys" chocolate — to be eaten after my breakfast of "bread-and-dip".

Seventy years is a long time, and I cannot now recall with any degree of certainty what those old books were. I think they must have been the "Sunday Herald" or the "Sunday at Home" — perhaps both. What I do remember is that they pushed ever so gently ajar the doors of a world from which no trumpet-call has ever been seductive enough to make worth-while any sort of repentant retreat. One story I remember to this day. It was called "Jessica's First Prayer", by Hesba Stretton.

I quoted earlier the first lines of Hood's "Past and Present". I end with the last:

> "It was a childish ignorance,
> But now 'tis little joy
> To know I'm farther off from Heaven
> Than when I was a boy."

Poor to-be-pitied poet! If only he had been able to share with me, at seven, my brave new Essex world, and to have come back, a lifetime later, to share with me the old! He would have found his heaven where, still cock-a-hoop on its shy little hill, I found mine. There were no sackbuts or psalms; no sinners, saints, principalities or powers. There were no golden gates, only white ones; but lettered in black across their width were words that quickened an ageing heart as, once upon a time, they had quickened a young one — "Scotts Farm."

CHAPTER TWO

Grandmother married twice and had nine children, five from the first marriage and four from the second. Her first husband was a William Pettit, the village blacksmith, who lived over his forge opposite the "Nag's Head". When he died, from what uncles and aunts euphemistically referred to as "The Fever", grandmother married again and moved with her new husband, a "Billy" Matthews, to Scotts Farm. Mother had been born at the smithy and, because of a twin loyalty to birthplace and "proper father", would now have nothing to do with either of them. She rebelled and fled to London where, in Upper Clapton, she became a "skivvy" to a chemist, his wife and four children under ten ("tea, sugar, beer and washing found. No followers or late nights"). It was like jumping out of the frying-pan and into the fire. Mother had been the oldest of the nine children and the habits of her girlish years had streaked with her into early womanhood. Now and then Father, in one of his less romantic moods, would call her a "cluckin' old 'en". I suppose in a way she was. When I enlisted in 1915 she flicked from my shoulder dust that was not there and told me for the umpteenth time always to make sure my underclothes were aired before I put them on and that, if ever I caught a cold, I was to rub a heart-shaped piece of brown paper (why brown?) with lard and clap it at once against my chest.

In addition to her wages of nine pounds a year as under-housemaid, Mother was given a supply of tallow candles. These were rationed to stop her staying up too late as, it would seem, the nine pounds were doled out for the same reason. For these she must (I quote from a "Servant's Manual" of the period) "sweep and dust the drawing-room before taking up the hot water. After this she must get her own breakfast and sweep down-stairs. Then she must make the beds and tidy the bedrooms. One day she must turn out her own bedroom and dressing-room, another day the spare room, another day the staircase, another day the bathroom, etc. Another day the two top spare rooms must be dusted — and the odd day can be occupied in mending. She will have entire charge of the bedrooms, seeing that hot water is there whenever required and that they are kept neat and tidy."

She was not happy in what Father called the "Gret Metrollops". Her room was an attic at the top of a flight of uncarpeted stairs. There was one brass-knobbed bed, one patchwork quilt, one faded reproduction of Landseer's "The Stag at Bay" and, in the darkest corner of all, one equally faded Sampler "worked by Janet Marsh in the year of our Lord, 1870, in the thirteenth year of her age." The Sampler read:

> "Preserve me, Lord, amidst the crowd,
> From every thought that's vain and proud,
> And raise my wand'ring eyes to see
> How good it is to trust in Thee."

In another corner there was a wash-hand stand, with one cracked jug, one cracked bowl, one cracked soap-dish, and one cracked toothbrush tray. There was no sign of one cracked anything else, and it was not until she had settled in that she found this under the bed, where she was daily adjured to let it remain. There was no telling when she might want to use it — "and we don't want the children woken up." It was "only decent" that the valance of the bed should cover its nakedness, just as it was only decent that an antimacassar should cover the nakedness of the legs of the piano in the drawing-room downstairs. A square of linoleum lifted lumpily from varnished boards and an unlockable door stood listening for the tinny commands of the bell beyond it on the landing. The door was so placed that Mother could open and close it whilst lying in bed.

Across the road, where the horse-buses and the hansom-cabs unwittingly primped away their little hour, was the Round Pond. Here the nursemaids wheeled their charges and the Young Ladies of Fashion showed as much of themselves as they dared. Mother hated it all and remembered Moreton. Even Father who, she knew, loved her in his rough-hewn way, gained by absence a halo that had never been his. She saw him at night, when the last day's chore was behind her and the house was blessedly still, thrown like a roguish star at the ceiling over her head by the gas-lamp on the pavement below. Sometimes he would be trudging back to Padler's End with water drawn from the pump in the yard between the "Nag's Head" and the school; at others he would be standing, as bold as a trumpet-call, in the square behind the "White Hart" where Mr. Jones of the Shop had his pigs slaughtered, waiting for the squeals and the blood and the scrubbing to stop and for that proud moment when the bladder, tied to a switch from the hedge, would be his to tease the girls with. Sometimes she would see him — as she had first seen him — scaring the crows for

18

sixpence a week with a clapper and a swinging row of potatoes stabbed with feathers.

He was clever with his hands. He could whittle skewers from dogwood (dogwood did not taint the meat) and shape clothes'-pegs from the willow before you could blink an eye. On the whatnot in her room at home was the pop-gun he had made from a piece of elder and the whistle he had made from a piece of sycamore. Each of them worked. He had hit a bottle at twenty feet with the gun and played "Sally in Our Alley" on the whistle — in correct tempo and tune. Mother had wanted to bring them with her, but her flight had been so headlong and unprepared. What she had brought (and what she kept near her pillow) was the Bible he had given her for her fourteenth birthday. On the fly-leaf he had written:

"John Charles Smith is my name,
England is my nation;
Moreton is my dwelling-place,
And   Christ is my salvation."

When the dust of her escapade had settled Father adventured to London to see her. The Great Northern was running an excursion for three shillings return between King's Cross and Skegness and he took Mother there for the day. It was a happy one for her but a sad one for him. "Come back!" he pleaded. But Mother had made up her mind. "I've got my pride," she said. That shattered his little world. What small talk he possessed thinned out to banalities and a foolish and mind-wasting dissertation on oats. "She must've thought I wer' tenpence in the shillin'," he later confessed.

Years later, when Father in turn came to London, they were married at the parish church of St. John-at-Hackney. I started to know him when he wrapped me in

19

the chenilled table-cloth from the kitchen and carried me into the Mafeking night of 1900 where near-demented men and women were tearing up the road's tarred blocks for bonfires. It was not so easy to get to know Mother. You had to storm through the savage shield of her love to plumb the rich depths which you knew were undoubtedly there. Her world had turned sour. What had she got for the Might-Have-Been? — the slums of Bethnal Green with, for full measure, a "wash'us" on the corner across the way and, overhead, where the missel-thrush should have been singing out his little heart to startle the dark mornings, steam-engines that guffawed day and night and spewed her country-white sheets with uncaring smuts.

She never complained. She moved about the repellent rooms of the poky flat with an unembarrassed graciousness that made people who met her for the first time think she was "too big for her boots." And she sang as she worked — hymns usually, different ones for different jobs. You always knew when the "Home Sweet Home" in the middle of the steel fender was getting its weekly application of emery cloth, for then she would sing:

"Underneath the gaslight's glitter,
Stands a fragile little girl,
Heedless of the night winds bitter,
As they round about her whirl;
While the hundreds pass unheeding,
In the ev'nings waning hours,
Still she cries with tearful pleading,
'Won't you buy my pretty flowers?' "

or when the brick copper in the "back-place" would not "catch" on washdays:

20

"Let us with a gladsome mind
Praise the Lord, for He is kind;
For His mercies shall endure
Ever faithful, ever sure,"

as if, by such frontal assault on the Almighty's vanity, she could woo him from his wondrous world and get him to breathe on the flame.

When Father got a better job we moved into a respectable house in a respectable street. The effect on Mother was almost beyond belief. She unpacked a case which since her flight had lain locked beneath her bed and sprinkled the rooms with waxed fruits, stuffed birds, china dogs and coloured glass. The windows she draped with the curtains she had made in the room over the road that dreamed up the slope from the humpbacked bridge at the foot of Ongar Hill, past the policeman's Essex-pink house and the post-office to the smithy on the corner. She even made her peace with the man who, so far, she had refused to acknowledge as her second father for, much to her delight, he brought the whatnot to town. She stared at it with tears in her eyes and doubt in her heart. But it was there, all right, topping a load of hay and complete with pop-gun and whistle! And she lost the chip on her shoulder. For years she had been an unresponsive audience to Father's reminiscences of their young days simply because her own had come to an untimely end and recital of them hurt. All that was over now. She turned with him the pages of an era that was more vitally alive than my own, its yesterday's men and women more clearly defined than today's, their arts and crafts and superstitions, their marriages, births and deaths, the things that had made them what they were. It was like listening to "The Thousand and One Nights".

You would not have thought that Mother, with her

demure little rosebud hats and a waist that Father could (and often did) span with his calloused hands, could have been a strict disciplinarian. She was. Especially where religion was concerned. On what she always referred to as the "One Day of Rest" it was Sunday School morning and afternoon and church at night — not forgetting God's ha'penny for the bag. At Easter there was Stainer's "Crucifixion" and three hours' twisting and turning for a soft bottom on a hard seat. When she thought I was old enough for her to know my own mind she talked to Father about presenting me to the Bishop of Stepney for Confirmation. That worried me; I was not holy enough. She did not argue. She bought me an Eton collar and a white silk tie and told me I looked like an angel.

* * * * * * * * * * *

Mother died, unofficially, on the 1st July, 1916, when my brother, Private Frederick Smith, 3rd Royal Fusiliers, was blown to bits on the Somme

"Part of him mud, part of him blood,
    The rest of him — not at all."

She died, officially, on the 13th January, 1969. Two days later, going through her effects, I found the Bible Father had given her. It fell open at the 23rd psalm where there was a folded sheet of time-stained paper. I prised it free of its creases and read for the first time, in Father's simple and blotted script, Browning's "Life in a Love". The first three words were heavily underlined: "Escape me? — Never!" I could not help smiling. I remember him telling me once: "When you git your 'ands on somethin' you love, boy, never let goo." He had been waiting behind the Pearly Gates all too long and now that he had again got his hands on something *he* loved he did not mean to "let goo" either. Mother had escaped him once; she was never going to escape him again — *ever*.

CHAPTER THREE

Much of what I did not learn myself when I stayed with grandmother and uncles and aunts in that explosive year of 1904 came from my Father. He confessed to being a "gormless gawk jist about able ter write me own name." That may have been partly true. I recall only two occasions when he put pen to paper: once when he completed a proposal form for the Hearts of Oak Benefit Society and once when, after saying, "I mus' tell the truth, boy," he notified My Lords Commissioners of the Admiralty that I was only seventeen years and three months old and not eighteen as I had earlier lied. Dear Father! His fight-against-time defence did not work. Having got hold of me, My Lords did not intend to relinquish me. They pushed me into the ranks of the Royal Marine Light Infantry and posted me, complete with King's Shilling and beef-sandwich, to Deal from where, three weeks later, with the help of a "high-up" at Whitehall, I was transferred to the Navy.

It would not have been necessary for Father to write the story of his life for you to know all about it. He had the most marvellous forget-me-not-blue eyes of any man I had known. They seemed to periscope from within every thought, word and deed that had ever been his, just as if, incapable of one-time escape and expression, those thoughts, words and deeds had etched themselves over a patient heart to await the right time for spelling them out to an impatient one. Except in rare moments of expansion Mother said little about the old life, but Father unleashed his memories with every meal. His starting-point was always with his own mother, "Owd Granny Smith", a remarkable woman who kept a still-room, a "Commonplace Book" and a barrel of rue tea outside the cottage door. She was famous for her frumenty, which she made by cooking wheat in milk and then boiling it up with cinnamon, honey and eggs, colouring the mixture with saffron "if ye eggs be pale". And, too, for her home-made wines: rhubarb, elderberry, blackcurrant and dandelion — even potato, parsnip and nettle. The potato wine was her "special" which she saved for the postman when the mornings were cold. "It wer' the nighest thing ter whisky I ever tasted," my Father used to say. "One glass o' thet an' yer wouldn't be knowin' whether 'twer Plough Sunday or Quinquagesima."

It was at Padler's End (once called Pedlar's End after the family of Christina Pedeluere) in the year of the penny-farthing and Hardy's "Under the Greenwood Tree', that my Father was born and where, at thirteen Owd Granny Smith, "mazed wi' a larnin' thet never filled nobody's stummick", removed him from school and hired him out for sixpence a week to scare with a clapper "they everlastin' crows". Father was not sorry to leave. He was a "pesky young muck", given to teasing the girls and smashing unlikely windows with his home-made catapult. The day before his last he had been found standing with hobnailed boots on the newly-scrubbed seat of the privy. He had been swiped on each hand with the cane and kept behind to clean it. After a spell on the land, he left Moreton to "better" himself. He got a job as a milk-boy at Loughton. The job did not last long. Home is where the heart is, and he moved back again to the land, picking up life where he left it, "knocking down ginger" when the nights were dark, and getting old ladies to lift voluminous skirts over stretched lengths of thread that were never there.

Halfway up the Ongar Hill was the field where he grew to love the Essex earth as unashamedly as he grew to love the girl living over the forge in Moreton. He was not much of a "scholard", but was an apt pupil. Soon he could hedge and ditch with the best of the "old uns". Ploughing took longer, but the day dawned when the gaffer himself praised him for straight furrows and a "good bit o' rainbow" at an "okkard" corner. Mother (who often sneaked over the bridge to peep at Father at work) thought he was best at sowing. With the seedlip slung on his left he would go up the furrows, scattering the seed with his right hand and, with it slung on his right, down them, scattering the seed with his left. It was not the easy thing it seemed. One change of step or of rhythm and the resultant bare patches would proclaim his incompetence. He had his own time for sowing, and only when he could "feel" the soil through his boots was it the right time. He would have been staggered to learn that someone in the sixteenth century had written: "Go upon the land that is plowed and if it synge or crye or make any noyse under thy fete then it is to wet to sowe. And if it make no noyse and will bear thy horses, thanne sowe in the name of Godd."

To Father, I think, Padler's End was Jack Hornerish pie into which every day he put a thumb and pulled out a plum. The world that fogged down upon him when he came to London to marry the girl who at home had slipped through his careless fingers, was not the real world. The real world was green with eternal springs and gold with eternal harvests. One spring had been greener than the rest, one harvest more golden. In the one he and the blacksmith's daughter had reached an understanding to "goo walkin' " and, in the other, he had been "shod". When a youngster harvested for the first time it was customary to hold him upside down and hammer the soles of his feet; then, to shouts of "He's shod! — he's shod!" he would be "brung uppards" and asked to pay his footing — usually a gallon of ale. The ceremony was known as "shoeing the colt".

Some of the men Father worked with remembered the "Horkey Bough". When the last sheaf had been pitched a horse would be harnessed to a branch of an oak tree. This would be wrenched off, hoisted to the top of the load and a toast drunk to it (the Horkey Bough) and the end of the harvest. One of the men, who had worked on the land "sin I wer' in me nine an' never 'ad no call ter be 'shamed on it," recalled that, "time I wer' a boy," one of his jobs was to place a green shoot on every tenth stook in the field. These stooks were "the ol' pusson's perks", which would later be collected in his own tithe wagon by the "ol' pusson" himself.

Much had been taken from the Essex Father had grown up in; much, however, remained. The flail was by no means dead, and where a farmer was too poor to hire "they gret ol' stim-ingins", it would often be brought into use. "It wernt a bad sort o' job", Father confessed. "It wer' in the dry an' matey-like. An' we didn't call the flail no fancy names, neither. We called it a 'stick-an'-an-arf'." This was because the handle was attaached by a leather hinge to a piece of blackthorn or yew half its length called the "swingle". Both woods were tough and did not splinter. As with scything, flailing was an art. An exhausting one, too. Experienced workers, rhythmically swinging in circles and figures-of-eight, would "kip on the goo" for hours, moving forward as a team, with one of them shovelling into sacks from time to time the accumulating grain for winnowing elsewhere.

Every Sunday over at Bovinger (not Bobbingworth, if you please!) there was the bell-ringing. Father was proud of this accomplishment and would have talked about it world without end if Mother, with an aiding-and-abetting twinkle in her eyes, had not pulled him down from his "high horse". He squeezed in his moments, all the same. "Clocking", I remember him telling me, was making the bell stand still and pulling the clapper against it with a rope, "chiming" was swinging the bell just enough to let the clapper strike the sound bow (whatever that was!), and "change-ringing" was — I grew to be as familiar with the words "Grandsire", Plain Bob" and "Stedman" as, over the years, I had grown to be familiar with the words of the "Lord's Prayer". Once, when Mother was cleaning out the canary's cage in the kitchen, I asked him if all that ringing didn't make his arms ache. "No," he said, "because—" Mother came in just as he was saying that because of the English way of ringing it had been found necessary to mount the bells higher between the gudgeons around which they rotated, and that — Mother left what she had to say till bedtime. Then she pecked Father on the forehead and, smiling at me, said, "Your grandad Pettit used to tell me to keep my big mouth shut till I knew enough to open it. You'd be wise to do the same. You know what your Father's like about bell-ringing. He knows all the answers; you don't."

It had not been all bell-ringing. There were things mysteriously referred to by Father as "ringers' jars", which evoked in Mother an unspoken acknowledgement but which left me in abysmal ignorance. I discovered later that they were, in fact, three-gallon or so earthenware containers with a handle at each side and a spigot at the

28

base. On New Year's Eve the ringers carried these containers to likely houses in the village, when wine, whisky, rum and other spirituous liquids were funnelled into them regardless. They were then taken back to the belfry and placed within easy reach of the ringers, who helped themselves whenever they felt like it.

Father believed that there was no point in being grown up unless now and again you could go back to being a child. There was that occasion when he bought a tricycle for my youngest brother. When it was delivered, dapple-grey and rubber-tyred, he took possession of it for three whole days, shifting the table against one of the walls and careering about like mad over the cheap linoleum that Mother so painstakingly polished every other day. His tastes were simple and few, a raw onion ("nothin' like it fer the complexion") and a crust of bread with his nightly glass of beer ("don't knock that over, boy; I'd sooner see the 'ouse fall down.") He had a "way" with that beer. When the weather was cold he "mulled" it, sticking the iron poker into the fire and plunging it when it was red-hot into it. Another of his loves was a clay pipe that was seldom out of his mouth. Mother hid the pipe when she was lucky enough to find it doing nothing on the mantelpiece or lying beside the enamel basin in the kitchen after he'd cleaned his teeth. It was impossible to keep the two separated for long. Father "sniffed it out" as he would have sniffed out a rabbit in a ten-acre field. There came a day, however, when it almost came to a sticky end. My younger brother and I dreamed home from the "flea-pit" one night, convinced that we could throw a lasso with the best of the cowboys we had just seen. Where could we demonstrate our prowess? We soon found out. The closet was at the bottom of the garden, end-on to the chicken-run. We cut Mother's clothes'-line in two and waited for Father to make the first move. He obliged sooner than we thought he might have done. We made what we thought was the right noose with the right running knot and climbed to the roof of the closet. Father had taken 'Lloyds Weekly News" with him, so it was a long time before we heard the cistern flush. When he emerged we whipped over the rope. It did not work. We had thought that the noose would clear his head and pinion his arms to his sides. All it did was to knock out his pipe from his mouth and send it flying. We had never seen Father so mad. Fortunately the pipe had fallen on soft ground. Father retrieved it, twiddled it gently between trembling fingers and plugged it back in his mouth. "Yer young buggers!" he stormed, "yer might 'ave bruk it!"

He quickly forgave, as he expected to be quickly forgiven, but the near-tragedy remained with him. Once, during the War, when he thought that every day might be my last, he recalled it. "Remember when —?" he began. His voice was a little uncertain, but he bravely went on. "I shouldn't 'a' bin so tetchy abowt it, boy," he finished, "but I wer' proud o' thet pipe. It took me nigh on a year ter git it thet colour." Then, shyly, like the boy he was, he drew me to him and kissed me. It was the first time he had ever done that.

London did its best to seduce him, but it never succeeded; his roots were too deep in that Essex soil which was home. Much of the old challenged and vanquished the new. Pictures were still "pickshers", chimneys still "chimbleys" — and what else could a snail have been but a "hodmedod"? Or what else Solomon's Seal but "Ladder to Heaven"? Or the White Convolvulus "Ol' Man's Nightcap"? Sometimes, when I was being "okkard", he would grip my wrist and say, "Do it agin if yer darst, boy!" and, much to Mother's amusement, he was always coming out with a "bit o' bren-butter" or "time fer fourses, ennit?". He remembered lots of those childish rhymes which had jingled, Lear-like, to every game he had ever played. Once he fitted a swing for my brothers and me in the doorway between what he called the "keepin' room" and the one that sheltered the aspidistra, reciting when he pushed us:

"Tittemy, tottemy, torter,
The ducks are on the water.
You goo UP, an' you goo DOWN,
Tittemy, tottemy, torter."

Years ago it had been the chorus of "Soldiers of the Queen", but as one particular session had ended disastrously for a cousin he had been sweet on (the swing had been dangerously near the bumbee-'ole and one of the ropes had parted at an inopportune moment), it had been blushingly discontinued.

Owd Granny Smith had been steeped in superstition, and much of it had rubbed off on him. Oddly enough, however, I can recall him resorting to it only once. That was when, while we were at dinner one day, a gypsy came to the door. Quick as a flash he leapt from his chair and slid a table-knife under the mat. "Thet'll frit 'im away," he grinned; "diddicoyes are feared o' steel." In many things Mother told him he was as obstinate as a mule. Nothing would convince him that the world was round and that it made one complete revolution every twenty-four hours. Neither was he deeply religious, though what religion he did have ran blade-straight and true through all the long years of his life. Hell was under his feet, in unfriendly earth, with heaven over his head in the clear blue sky — not that he could be sure of the last; he hoped it would come as a pleasant surprise. He subscribed to a love that bore all things, believed all things, hoped all things, and endured all things — but there was a limit. When he prayed it was because he wanted something, and when he thanked God it was because he had got it. I know that over and over again he thanked God for having been born in Essex. His one great regret was that I had not been born there, too. Still, you could not have everything. I was born in London, within the sound of Bow Bells. That made me a cockney which, he supposed, was the next best thing.

(I wonder . . .)

When, on his seventieth birthday, he said, "The trouble wi' folk these days is thet they look forrard too much an' backards too little", Mother tweaked his ear and reminded him that there was still a candle on the cake that wanted blowing out. She doubtless appreciated the significance of the remark but, like the down-to-earth woman she was, knew that there was a time and place for everything. I had reached one of my own birthdays before it meant anything to me; then, with one colossal burst of resolution, I pelted down to Padler's End where, for "one far fierce hour and sweet", I was determined at long, long last to look "backards" with my Father.

I did not go into Moreton — I would have broken down and cried — but took the long way round to Padler's End, past the place where Father was born and then on to the church where, all those crumpled years ago, he had pulled the beloved ropes of his beloved bells. Time had stood still for it. The clerk's desk was as he would have remembered it; so was the pulpit, enriched with its elaborate and intricate carving; so was the big 17th century chest with its four hopeful slots for money. I knelt and prayed — I do not know what — with that peace which the world cannot give all around me. Then I came out to a June afternoon as sweet as a nut. I walked slowly back. The trees were top-heavy with leaf and a few woolly clouds lolled fatly content in the sun. On the

Padler's End side of the bridge the breast-high signpost whispered in challenging black that up the dreaming hill beyond was Moreton. The hill pricked me with the points of a memoried womb in Time that was mine yet was not mine. How often, in those unhurried years when every day was the Sabbath, had my Father climbed it? How often, hand-in-hand with his "English rose", had he come down it? On the farther bank of the stream was the willow which had sheltered them while he formed for her with deft fingers pop-guns from the hollow-stemmed elder and "squirts" from the shoots of sheep's parsley; and from which, when shadows were slanting to tell the time and lamps were waiting to smudge impatient windows, he had led her back to the forge. Their world was young and as exciting as a locked door, with 1914 as distant as the remotest star.

* * * * * * * * * * *

Somewhere in an English churchyard is a gravestone which reads "Dere Childe!" and somewhere in a Kipling poem is the verse:

"Teach us delight in simple things,
And mirth that has no bitter springs;
Forgiveness free of evil done,
And love to all men 'neath the sun."

Both would have stuck in Father's throat like Macbeth's "Amen!" — but both would have fitted him "proper'n a glove."

33

CHAPTER FOUR

When I think back to Scotts Farm I think back to quaint
little rooms, crooked passages and tilting ceilings so low
that I found myself ducking my head with every
crusading step. I fell in love at first sight and knew, as
soon as I sniffed its smells, that it was going to make me
better. There was no *angularity* about it — if I can put it
like that — just a shape that made a cosy fit and left no
bulges or bumps. Even the clocks — and there were lots
of them — ticked "Welcome". And they were all so
happily right. You never got the feeling that half of you
was in yesterday and that half of you was in tomorrow.
Grandmother carved me a thick slice of bread and
smothered it with lard and soft brown sugar. "Git thet
inside yer," she said, "an' then be off. But tek care o' they
motey-cars; they're gittin' ter these parts now."

I made a "Cook's Tour" of the stables and sheds,
creaked open the door of the barn and squinted inside,
and then went on to the dairy. I liked this. It was white
and cool and gurgled with milk. At four in the afternoon
the villagers brought their jugs here to be filled for a
penny. If they had "forgotten" their pennies — as often
they had — grandmother saw to it that the jugs were filled
just the same. Then I "lifted" a greengage from the tree in

34

the orchard, and swaggered out on to the road. Here there was a triangle of grass with a signpost pointing to the Roothings and, opposite the triangle, a field called "Three Gates". I had good reason to remember this. When grandfather thought I was strong enough to stand on my own " two fit", he thrust a double-barrelled rifle at me and told me to fire at a rabbit. I did. The rifle recoiled, knocked me flat on my back and sent me to bed for the next three days with abrasions and shock. Grandmother had "no mind" for rabbits, but cooked them in wine for the men, warning them beforehand to be careful of the lead shot they were invariably peppered with. "Yer don't want cannon-balls rattlin' abowt in yer stummicks, do yer?" Rabbits were good "filler-uppers", but stuck to the ribs like glue. This could also be said for the plain roly-poly she brought to the table on Sundays. Cut into thick slices and swimming in gravy you could have stood a spoon in, it was served before the meat. Not that you wanted the meat very much.

I had other reasons for remembering "Three Gates". It was where I saw my first mushrooms and my first fairy-ring. It was where, too, I tried to kiss one of my cousins. She was not flattered. She said, "Soppy thing!" and pushed me backwards into a ditch. Grandfather had no love for the field. There was a footpath (he called it a "dool") from the gates to the back of the cottages opposite the church, and people from Fyfield way were always using it as a short cut. He snorted when I made a suggestion. 'Yer can't close a field thet's got a footpath, any more then yer kin close one thet's 'ad a corpse carried over it. It's agin the law." I do not think that anything "agin the law" would have worried grandfather. He hated the indoor life and often "slept rough" — not always soberly. Sometimes he had been brought home by the police and sometimes by one or another of his men. No one doubted his kind heart, but you had to get used to him. He had mahogany-brown skin, a roving black beard, and wore a corduroy suit, a billycock hat and buskins that buttoned at the side. When you had got used to him you would find that he liked the Preludes of Chopin and that, on Sunday afternoons, he bribed one of my cousins to play the piano and me to tickle his stockinged feet with a teaspoon. For this unusual ploy he would give my cousin a penny and me a promise to take me with him to market one day. One day the promise materialised. I shall never forget the experience — the clip-clop of old "Dobbin" through the long dark night, the carriage-lamps blobbing with yellow light the dog-rose hedges of North Weald, Epping and Woodford and, at journey's end, the dawn breaking out like a rash over Stratford and the hay-market at Aldgate. Till then I had never known what dreams there could be on top of a load of hay.

Father said that grandmother must have been "off 'er rocker" to marry him. Maybe yes, maybe no. She was certainly an amazing woman; a great patriot, too. My country, right or wrong! On the wall over the mantelpiece in the parlour were pottery plaques of the "Old Queen" and her Consort with, on each side of them, portraits of Gladstone and Disraeli. The mantelpiece itself was a jungle of crimson lustres, photographs, and two discoloured ostrich eggs hooped with silver. I did not like the ostrich eggs; they made me feel sad. What I did like was something called, I think, a "polyphon", a squarish box that played with steel combs perforated metal discs. Two of the songs I particularly liked were "Will ye no come back again?" and "Annie Laurie" - though why, in the last, any sane man would want to lay himself "doon and dee" for someone whose brow was like the "snaw-drift", I was never able to understand.

36

Grandmother was a "queen" herself, second in importance only to the vicar. Once, when she was bending over the washtub, she called out, "Yer'd think I was allus smellin' o' Sunlight Soap an' a line o' white washin', wouldn't yer?" When the need arose she could doll herself up and be as presentable as a crinolined countess. The vicar relied on her to grace the Church Ales that were sometimes held in his spacious grounds and, when a "special do" was to be given in the village hall, she would be invited to sit where she could be seen and admired. All this seemed a little alien to the real granny Matthews. She would dock a lamb without demur because, if she did not, the fat would run to its tail, yet, a minute or so later, would reprimand one of the hands for destroying a martin's nest because it was unlucky. Like most of the villagers she was superstitious. To have put an even clutch of eggs under a broody hen would have been to court disaster; either the eggs would not hatch out or, if they did, the birds would be all cockerels. She was even superstitious about the butter she was famous for. It would not set until she had dropped into it a spoonful of water from the well in "Back Medder". Nor would it set if she failed to croon over it:

> "Come, butter, come,
> Come, butter, come;
> Peter's standing at the gate,
> Waiting for a buttered cake;
> Come, butter, come."

My cousins and I were always sure of a taste of that butter when, on each of her birthdays, we lined up to give her our presents. She would spread a golden knob over a hot dumpling and then sprinkle the dumpling with sugar. It was delicious.

37

3A

A frequent visitor to Scotts Farm was my aunt Maude. She had married uncle Will, one of my grandmother's sons by her first marriage and, later, the union not working out as it should have done, had become governess to a wealthy family in Eaton Square. She was given to admonitions of "Master John would not have said" (or done) "that" whenever my cockney traits lifted through the thickening veneer of a burgeoning Essex existence. She was prim, proper and pedantic, steering the craft of a foreign life by the grammatical star of "the right word in the right place". One day, when even the shadows looked as if they had taken a bath, she glanced over my shoulder at a letter I was writing. She fanned her thin fingers over it and said, "Charles, dear, you're not treating your sentences as you should. You must learn to *caress* them, then they will end by smiling at you." That was enough to nullify her do's and don'ts and rocket her to the top of my list of loves, but when, later, I found she had filched the advice from Anatole France, she plummeted with the speed of light to its bottom. Mother would have approved the relegation; she did not like aunt Maude — she was too "high-faluting", the sort of woman who goes to the closet with "Twinkle, twinkle, little star", and comes out with:

"Up above the world so hay,
Lake a day-a-mand in the skay."

I have always been suspicious of happiness; it is like a balloon — inflate it too much and it bursts. Mine burst when I started school, and that

" . . . sweet contentment
The countryman doth find"

shrivelled and zig-zagged to my boots. There was a

38

reason. I was a "furriner", with thin legs, a chalk-white face and an accent which stuck out a mile. And my name (which Mother said meant strong and manly) did not help. There were chants of:

"Ol' Charlie-wag! Ol' Charlie-wag!
Ate the pudden and gnawed the bag!"

which compelled me in the end to seek the safe shelter of a nettled cubby-hole at the back of the school not normally used for tears.

Grandmother seemed not to notice my dejection when I arrived back home. She gave me my tea and then, when I had finished moping under the greengage tree, told me it was time for the "wooden 'ill". In the bedroom that looked down the road to the church, after I had charged the length of a weepy "God-bless-Mum-and-Dad-and-make-me-a-good-boy-Amen", she divested me of my velvet sailor suit, my high buttoned boots and the lace collar that Mother so lovingly flat-ironed and which I was so proud of, and stowed them away in the tallboy. 'Yer won't be needin' this lot agin," she said grimly, "'cept, mebbe, fer 'igh days an' 'olidays." In the morning, on the chair by the side of the bed, lay a bar of nougat and a workaday suit of my cousin Frank, complete with a pair of stout, but sensible, shoes. The alchemy paid off. By the time we had finished the hymn "New every morning is the love -" Charlie-wag had gone for ever, and I was "one o' they".

CHAPTER FIVE

School . . .

This was a one-storey building separated from the flinty road by a railed-off playground and from the "Nag's Head" by an open space in the middle of which stood the village pump. Forty or so of us — "Mixed Infants" as we were somewhat doubtfully dubbed — scrambled morning and afternoon into the one large classroom and sat on backless forms facing a master with a voice that sometimes sounded like the one that had breathed o'er Eden or, sometimes, when our ignorance or behaviour plagued him, like the Brigade of Guards. We liked him, though. When he laughed his face threatened to splinter into a thousand tinkling stars. Education was primitive, but sound: reading, writing and arithmetic, with snippets of history — 1066 and all that — supplemented by charts as yellow as Time itself. And we used slates, with slate pencils that screeched like souls in torment and made me ache in every tooth. The pencils were a mixed blessing. Sometimes, when they required sharpening, those of us who were monitors took them outside and rubbed their points against the soft yellow brick of the porch, "working to rule" if the lesson we had escaped from was one we did not like.

There was no further hostility against me; I had been "accepted". But I was still "the bo-o-y from Lunnon" who, with an aura about him of a city as mystic and remote as Samarkand, had come to shame them as "scholards". They need not have worried; I was kept under the watchful eye of the headmaster who balanced to a hair's breadth the scales of Scholastic Justice and who was, as we used to say, "not so dusty, well-brushed". We had a verse for him which was not our own but which had been handed down to us:

"Mr. Gordon's a very good man,
He goes to church on Sunday;
He prays to God to give him strength
To cane us boys on Monday."

We had other verses, too (not part of the school curriculum), verses which fixed in our minds for all time subjects which otherwise might have been difficult to learn. There was this, for instance, about the Ten Commandments:

"Thou shalt have no God but me,
Nor unto idols bend the knee.
Take not the name of God in vain,
Nor dare the Sabbath to profane.
Give to thy parents honour due,
And never shalt thou murder do.
In every word and deed be clean.
Steal not, for thou of God art seen.
Speak thou the truth, and always love it.
Thy neighbour's goods thou shalt not covet."

And this, about the twelve apostles:

41

"Twelve apostles were chosen, and their names
Were Andrew, Peter, John and James,
Thomas and Bartholomew,
Matthew and Philip, too,
James the lesser, and Jude the greater,
Simon the Zealot, and Judas the traitor."

Sometimes the vicar paid us an appraising visit. He was a slight old man, as ancient as the hills, who pedalled the rutted roads on a tricycle and whose eyes were so bad that he saluted even the stumps of trees under the impression that they were his parishioners. He wore a black cape and a black broad-rimmed hat that flapped in the slightest breeze like a raven's wing. His services were sparsely attended because, I suppose, he was only *in* the church, like the stained-glass windows, and not *of* it. And he always seemed to be in a hurry, with his "Glory - be - to - God - the - Father - God - the - Son - and - God - the - Holy - Ghost" gusting from his lips like a streamer in the wind. You somehow sensed that a country pulpit was not the best place to be comfortable in and that back at the vicarage there was a cosy fire and a dish of buttered crumpets. My Father had been a choirboy at the church (St. Mary's) and had written in the Bible he later gave to Mother: "Shortest verse: John XI,35 — Jesus wept; shortest psalm: 117 — 2 verses; number of letters: 3,556,480."

The playground, where we sucked like mad the humbugs and aniseed balls we bought with our farthings at the Two Miss Prentices, was the be-all and end-all of school. There we staged our games: hop-scotch, marbles, conkers ("Obli onker, my first conker"), whip-top, tag, the king's horses, kissing-in-the-ring and skipping — "salt, mustard, vinegar, PEPPER!" There was one game that led to my undoing. A boy sat with parted legs with a screw on its head between them. The rest of us, one by one, tried to topple the screw with cherry-stones. The stones which missed became the property of the boy with the screw. When I had won some hundreds one of my class-mates told me that if I took them to Ashdown's, the drapers, in Ongar, they would buy them from me for dolls' eyes. I rose to the bait like a fish. One Saturday morning I washed and polished my hoard and then, without a word to a soul, trudged on my thin legs the three dusty miles to the town that I thought would be my Klondyke. Mr. Ashdown considered my offer with an outward and visible grace and what I now suspect was an inward and invisible sense of fulfilment. He beamed and asked, "Where's your gran, then?" When I told him that gran was at home making jam he walked me to the door and tweaked my ear. "There, boy," he grinned, "now run home and learn to be less gullible." The incident was not without its sequel. After lessons on Monday there was a fight in the field behind the school. I came out of it with a black eye and the glib Ananias with a bloody nose. Mr. Ashdown would have applauded both.

Grandmother was a woman of the first importance at Ashdown's. When she had ordered her meat at Carter's, the butcher's, at the bottom of the town, she would shop there for her linens. Mr. Ashdown himself would serve her, washing his hands in invisible soap and bringing out the port wine and biscuits. A packet of pins (often given away when there was a farthing in the change) or an expensive frock was all the same to Mr. Ashdown; Mrs. Matthews was — well, Mrs. Matthews was Mrs. Matthews, wasn't she? It intrigued me when grandmother ordered a yard of this-that-or-the-other. Mr. Ashdown would conjure down from the shelves a huge roll of cloth and, with one dexterous forefinger, whip it the whole long length of the counter.

We were not all "regulars" at school. Some of the boys played truant to ply their rattles bird-scaring in the fields and some of the girls went pea- or bean-picking with their mothers. The money came in handy. Rents were low, the cost of living was low, and most of the villagers kept a pig or two and grew their own vegetables, but the average weekly wage was in the region of twelve shillings, not much when you took into account the number of children per head.

Opposite the school, on the corner, was the blacksmith's. I felt at home there. It had belonged to grandfather Pettit and Mother had been born in one of the rooms above it. In a way, in those pre-natal days when, as Mother prettily put it, I was God's, it had belonged to me, too. Certainly it had belonged to me at five. Mother lived in a Past that was the Present, the Future and the Great Hereafter, smoothing every day one painted word after another over a canvas already tangy with smoke, saliva, droppings and sweat, and furnishing me with a forge as recognisable as my own pallid features. It was a magical place of gloom and ghosts and cobwebby distances lit by the dancing flames of the furnace; all the more magical when, as a special treat, we were let in to hold a box of nails or hand to Mr. Pain a hammer-like tool he called the "pritchell".

Mr. Pain was a little man with a big son, Harry. Harry stuttered. Whenever he saw me going to school, or leaving it, or trying to hoist myself over the half-door of the smithy, he would call "Cha-Cha-Cha-*Char*-lee!" much as he might have cluck-clucked a bantam cock before scattering its feed of corn. The stutter did not affect his artistry as a craftsman or, indeed, as a purveyor of knowledge. He told me what I already knew, that the frills round the bottom of the blacksmith's apron were to stop scales from the glowing iron dropping on to the anvil

44

and spoiling his work. He had only to bunch the apron and there was a ready-made brush with which to sweep the anvil clean. He told me, too, what I did not know, that the cobwebs high on the rafters were not destroyed because they caught the flies which otherwise would have fidgeted the horses and made shoeing more difficult than it was. One hot and slow Sunday morning, when he was slanting his way from the "Nag's Head", he posed me this:

"Father, mother, sister, brother
Ran all day and couldn't catch each other.
What are they?"

I said I did not know. He giggled. "The spokes of a waggon wheel."

He was a good workman, but not as sensitive as his father. He, before he laid so much as a finger against a horse, thrilled to the nearness of coronet, fetlock, pastern and heel, as once on a time he had thrilled to the nearness of a face that had been his happy sunrising. There was nothing pretty about them, he knew, but ugliness was a point of view. An ulcer was a lovely thing to a pathologist.

Mr. Pain was the most important man in the village. He made, as well as shoes, all sorts of tools: bill-hooks, forks, harrows, plough-spuds, drills and shears; and put an edge that would last on all sorts of cutting instruments: sickles, scythes, axes and hoes—even the odd pair of scissors that the poorer mums wrapped in a page of the "News of the World" and smuggled at night via a hot little hand to the door of his house. Sometimes the farmers brought wheels to be retyred. A thick ribbon of iron was heated and shaped to a circle. This, after being left to cool, was reheated over a wood fire and hammered while still hot over the rim of the naked wheel clamped to a tyre-ring on the brick floor. Buckets of water were then flung over it to make the tyre contract and so bind the felloes to each other and the spokes to the hub. These were the moments of sound and fury.

"Bliss was it in that dawn to be alive,
But to be young was very heaven."

One of the highlights of school was the 24th May, Empire Day. We were assembled in front of a wall-map smutched with splodges of faded red. Mr. Gordon pointed them out as if they were his. "This, and this, and this," he said, "is the British Empire, the Empire on which the sun never sets." Then, like the patriots we were, we marched with heads held high into the playground to recite as much as we could remember of Kipling's "Recessional" and salute the Union Jack. It was a proud moment. We could not have guessed that, in our own lifetime, that Empire would have disintegrated like Rome's, and that we would be thinking back to:

"Beneath whose awful Hand we hold
Dominion over palm and pine"

and mumbling instead:

"Far-called, our navies melt away;
On dune and headland sinks the fire:
Lo, all our pomp of yesterday
Is one with Nineveh and Tyre!"

It was Kipling who foresaw the end of Empire. He knew, as we know now, that you cannot teach a man all you have learnt and then expect to hang on to the goods and chattels you stole from him when he was ignorant. It is all so pitiful. To me in those days there was something

46

ennobling in being an Englishman. Perhaps, having lived through what our children and grandchildren will never have the good fortune to live through, I am a fuddy-duddy. My eyes still blink with tears when I hear at a Promenade Concert Elgar's "Land of Hope and Glory". I am not ashamed to make the confession. I would rather be a rusticating Royalist than a revolutionary Roundhead. Any old day of the week.

One summer night every year the Woodford Meet gathered outside the forge to start their journey home. Their cycles were festooned with Chinese lanterns and ribbons of coloured paper, so that the road between the "Nag's Head" and the "White Hart" looked as if it had been taken over by all the painted glow-worms of all Essex. With tinkling bells and bobbing lights they sped down the slope past Jones's, the stores, and the one-man police station, and then up and over the hump-backed bridge. We watched them climb the Ongar Hill till they were lost to sight and the chimes of their bells could be heard no more. Then we ourselves left, the women and children for their oil-lamps and their sweating floors and the men for their pubs and their staling beer. At that particular moment of loss darkness had never been more profound or sadness more poignant.

I suppose that one of life's greatest gifts is that of being able to say: "I'm happy — *now*". Perhaps if I had been old enough to possess the gift myself I might that night have sandwiched those lovely lines of Henry Charles Beeching between my gabbled "God-bless-Mum-and-Dad-Amen!" and my last lingering look over fields that would sleep till tomorrow became another day:

> "God who created me
> Nimble and light of limb,
> In three elements free,

47

To run, to ride, to swim;
Not when the sense is dim,
But now from the heart of joy,
I would remember Him —
Take the thanks of a boy."

Perhaps, even now, it is not too late to ask Him to take
the thanks of a man . . .

CHAPTER SIX

When it was wet my cousins and I played in the "studio", a large hut-like building once used by an artist. Then it was stacked with sacks of potatoes. We used to chip the bad ones up and weigh them out on toy scales. Sometimes, when we could not get potatoes, we weighed up the cocoa-brown earth from around the roots of the greengage tree and sold it as sugar. One morning, when I was alone, grandmother came in and said that if I were good I could go down after tea to Moreton Fair. I hugged her with such ferocity that the jet brooch she had been wearing since the death of Queen Victoria unpinned itself and fell to the floor. The fair, a STUPENDOUS ATTRACTION, was an event which villagers for miles around supported, attended and enjoyed. I was a cockney, but I meant to support, attend and enjoy it, too. As soon as tea was over and grandmother had brushed the last speck of dust from my clothes, I pushed along the beautiful but overgrown North Lane on the corner till I came out to the road that led to the "tin" chapel. This was where some of my less disciplined C. of E. uncles and aunts attended when they felt like a post-service drink at the round-the-corner "Pig and Whistle".

To the right of me was "Crispins" and, beyond it, the post mill (now demolished) where, when my Mother was

49

a girl, she had carried "gleanings" to be ground. A short distance from the mill was "Poppin House" and, farther along, what we called (for no reason that we knew of) "the Merrikees". My cousins and I gave them a wide berth. Early one morning one of my uncles had found a dead man there. He had fallen — apparently asleep — from the top of a load of hay and, one foot trapped in the noose of a rope, had been dragged for miles over the feelingless flinty road. A little way down on the left, almost opposite "The Lindens", was the sawpit. This was operated by the two men who, I think, owned it. The man who worked on top like a bearish Blondin said "Marnin'" and "Ev'nin'" and, once in a while, when he was in a happier mood: "Th' ol' moon's bin on 'er back all night; likely we're in fer the floods", but seldom anything else. His mate Chuck, small, bright as a button, and with a face as shiny as one of grandmother's suet "puddens", wore a threadbare shirt, "trowsis" strapped below the knees with "wallies" and, because he had found it in the vicarage dustbin, what he called his "Thenks-be-ter-Gawd" hat, a mangy black thing that kept the sandy drifts of sawdust out of his eyes. He seemed to like me. Whenever he saw me in my lanyarded sailor suit he would freeze to a standstill, lift his face to a sky he knew as well as the back of his hand and shout, "Out wi' the buntin', mate! One lord 'igh bluddy admiral comin' aboard." Sometimes, when there was an audience, he would sing:

> "*Pull* for the shore, sailor,
> *Pull* for the shore;
> '*Eed* not the rollin' wave,
> But *cling* to the oar"

underlining each word coinciding with the beginning of his downward stroke of the saw. He had no voice to speak of, but it made his day to think that people came to hear him sing rather than to be in at the death of a craft.

The fair was held in a field half-way between the Corner Houses and the field that pushed out a nervous path from its own gate to the gate a dozen hilly yards from the "Pig and Whistle". I was all of a birthday bubble and my knees shivered as a hungry horse's will shiver when its feed-bag is about to be slung over its head. It was already getting dark and I could glimpse above the squiggles of the trees the first faint flickers of the dripping naphtha flares and hear dropping from the colouring skies the lusty guffaws of the merry-go-round. And then — oh, then! — I was in, mud over the buckles of my patentleather shoes and a splinter from the machine-scarred gate in one of my hands.

The first thing I bought was a "lady's tickler", a feather from a peacock's tail tied to the end of a twig. It was a good investment, an "Open Sesame!" that gave the boy the status of the man. I had lots of pennies, but there was so much to be seen and done that it was difficult to know in what order they should be disposed of. I fought shy of the hoop-la. There was a watch there that Father would have been proud to show to his mates, and a gold bangle that would have made Mother's pretty arms prettier still. But it would have been throwing money away. They, in common with the rest of the "jewellery", had been expertly positioned on wood squares which it was impossible for the hoops to clear and so lie flat on the stall. A few feet away my uncle Frank was bowling for the pig. He stopped to give me the thumbs-up sign and sixpence, which I spent on brandy-snaps, ginger-bread, a toffee-apple and a cold saveloy. I now felt cocky enough to dare the challenge of "The Fattest Woman in the World".

51

The cockiness was short-lived. I was singled out on the edge of the crowd by the "barker". "Arf price fer you, young gent," he called, pushing the rim of his top-hat towards me. "An no extry charge fer pinchin' the lovely lady where she don't wanna be pinched." I felt hot and ashamed and prayed that none of my cousins, uncles or aunts had seen me. There was an oblong corridor of night between the rifle-range and the Aunt Sally booth, and I trembled along its leavening length till it hid me from a world I had so basely betrayed. I was still sobbing when a voice came out of the darkness. It belonged to "Gritty" Noakes. "Thought it wer' yew, boy" he said. "Bin doin' summat yew shouldn't 'ev bin?" He led me into the light. "Let's goo an' git a drink. I'm thet thusty I could knock a pub back. 'Sides, I got summat fer yer, like I said." I followed him into the refreshment tent where he bought a still lemonade for me and a bottle of beer for himself. Then he fished into one of his pockets and pulled out a piece of wood, flat like a breakfast-plate and heavily notched around its edge. "Like I said," he repeated, "— the bull-roarer I promised yer. Swing it round yer 'ead wi' the string an' the folks in the chuch'll think it's Judgement Day."

Gritty (who could swear "suthin' 'mazin' " when he wanted to) was the roadman. Straight as a telegraph pole and as thin as a rasher of wind, he had three loves: his "baccy", his pipe, and the conical piles of grit at the side of the roads from High Laver bridge to Scotts Farm, and from the forge to the summit of Ongar Hill where the sandpits were. He watched over the grit like a threeheaded Cerberus, and neither Orpheus with his lute nor Sibyl with her cake of honey and poppies could have wooed him from it. He never "ailed". "I dunno what thet rheumatiz is they goo on abowt," he once confessed, "I never 'ev it. I swallers me mum's rue tea, an' walks

52

round a flock o' ship ev'ry day. Me dad allus did it, an' what kep 'im 'ale an' 'earty kips me 'ale an' 'earty, too." He finished his drink and we left the tent for the enamelled night. Then, so suddenly that it almost hurt, he pressed my hand and, with a wry twist of his lips, said, "Bless ye, boy! — an' don't never 'ev nuthin' ter do wi' no wimmin ever agin. They ent wuth it — any on 'em — thin 'uns *or* fat 'uns." Then, like a flash, he was off.

Gritty's gentle revelation of what I took to be a mutual defection from village propriety sent me away rejoicing. I straddled a mangy mare on the merry-go-round with the devilry of one of the six hundred who, not so long ago, had galloped into the jaws of death and into the mouth of hell; I cavorted on the cake-walk, hurtled down the helter-skelter, and well-nigh swooned on the swings. I was now so unafraid of life that I almost denounced as a fraud the cheap-jack who, when he sold you a purse, "palmed" the half-crown he pretended to drop into it as part of your "bargain" and slipped it into his pocket instead. I crossed to the coconut shy, where I stood "arf-way fer boys an' gels", and pitched a couple of movable objects towards a dozen or so immovable ones; then, disgusted, I tried the stall where you had to knock down with a rag ball a pyramid of empty tins. I shall never know what happened, but I demolished three lots of tins with three successive balls. "Lucky little perisher!" grumbled the woman and gave me a sea-sicky vase which I dumped in an unresponsive ditch on the way home.

By this time I was getting thirsty again. There was a man near the gate selling glasses of sarsaparilla which, he declared, for one copper coin of the realm would give you a complexion as lovely as that of "Her Late Lamented Majesty — God Bless Her!" I decided to take no chances and bought two. I do not think the stuff did anything for my complexion, but it certainly did something for the rest of me. I tickled one of the rectory's prim maids, giggled when a water-squirt misfired into my face and, doughtily daring, went back to stare again at the fat woman's tent. The lights seemed brighter, the noises more clamorous. I felt as if I were contained in a crazy cathedral where nothing could get in and nothing could get out. When, presently, uncle Frank found me, he gave me a queer old look and said, "Time we wer' gittin' back, boy. Yer gran'll be clanjanderin' else an' yer'llbe slippin' under the bed wi' the china." He had won the pig, he said, and was going to collect it in the morning.

We were both tired when we reached the farm. Grandmother said there was no need to ask if I had enjoyed myself — she could see I had, "yer young muck!" — and carried me up the stairs to bed. I awoke with the sun brindling my bed and the smell of bacon and eggs. Grandmother kissed me and said, "Yer uncle Frank's bin an' gone. 'E tol' me ter gi' yer this." She handed me a parcel. I unwrapped it with fingers that were all thumbs — and there on the table was the silver watch and the gold bangle. When Gritty left me he had met uncle Frank and unfolded my story. Uncle Frank, who by this time had won the pig, charged over to the hoop-la stall and persuaded the man to agree to a swap. It was as simple as that.

Dear Gritty! Dear uncle Frank! The watch was not silver and the bracelet was not gold, but they must have been precious. When a few days later my parents came to see me and I made the "presentations", Mother wept and Father blew his nose into a spotted handkerchief that Mother had often said no respectable person would have been found dead with. It was a heart-warming end to a heart-warming occasion, and one I frequently look back to. Especially do I think back to the unknown quantity, "The Fattest Woman in the World". "Pinch the lovely

54

young lady where she don' wanna be pinched." It was a "dare" I could have got away with, a dare I could have cherished with pride in my greying years. Young or old, short or tall, blonde or brunette, a Beauty or a Beast? I shall never find out. I never knew her, or saw her or, even, pinched her, but for me, at seven, she topped the bill and stole the show . . .

CHAPTER SEVEN

A wise old Italian once remarked: "Misfortune does not always come to injure." How right he was! If I had not gone down with that bronchitis and double pneumonia I might never have known as a boy my parents' Essex and that multitude of uncles and aunts who, turn and turn about with grandmother, nursed me to health.

My favourite was aunt Daisy, then living opposite the school. She was one of three sisters (aunt Maude was one) who had married three of Mother's brothers. Later she moved to "Brook Lodge" at the High Laver end of Moreton. "Brook Lodge" had once been the "Pig and Whistle". It was more "stuck-uppish" than the cottage left empty behind in Church Road. And more remote. The gypsies would call there now and then with tales of hard luck, chalking the gates with a Romany "curse" if the call was without effect; but for the pedlars and packmen it was off the beaten track. Their "shop" was the village, where they displayed their remarkable range of wares — shirt buttons, laces, studs, reels of cotton and thread and the like — as reverently as they might have displayed the Crown Jewels. One of them (" 'Arry of 'Oxton" he called himself) was a plausible spieler who often reduced me to tears. "Look, lady," he would say, "if

I could let you 'ave it cheaper, I would, but I got a big wife and three small kids to feed. 'Ere! tell you what. As you're my best customer I'll cut me losses and let you 'ave it fer arf price. Can't say no fairer'n that, can I?". Then, without more ado, he would wrap the article up and thrust it into the woman's hands before she had time to change her mind.

Another "regular" was "Mogga". He was a gangling sort of man with steel-rimmed spectacles. We called him "four-eyes". He did not seem to mind, perhaps because of his clerical absorption. There was a pen behind his ear and a bottle on string round his neck. Whenever he sold anything he teased out the pen, prised out the cork and dipped the pen into the bottle. Having recorded the sale in a little green book he replaced the cork and pen and surveyed his clientele with magnified eyes and as much loving-kindness as he might have shown to a faltering ballerina. The procedure thinned the profits but left the leisurely Mogga happy in mind, body and estate. In 1904, when all the world was young, he had another ten years to go before he was to stop standing and staring. Not to worry . . .

The wet fishmonger came on Fridays. He was aggressively short, with a stomach as comfortably round as one of his barrels, and weighed on scales that went down with a generous bump mackerel, herrings, soles and plaice, but not without wiping them first down an apron rigid with grime and grease. His van was covered from front to back with a black canvas hood on which was daubed in white the price of everything dead or dying beneath it. In large capitals were the words "FRESH GOD". He grinned mischievously when twitted about them by people not in the know. "Good fer trade", he said. "No one'd notice else."

It was a great day when the "Vinegar Man" came. Not

only did he sell vinegar, but pots and pans, carbolic soap, "Monkey Brand" ("Won't wash clothes"), Oakey's emery powder, crockery, mousetraps, brickdust, even pens:

"They come as a boon and a blessing to men:
The Pickwick, the Owl and the Waverley pen"

— all from a cart no bigger than a hay-waggon. He loved children. When we were sent with "mouldies" and "mites" for hearthstones or triangular blocks of salt he would wrap them in pages from "Alley Sloper's Half Holiday" or the "Golden Penny". Sometimes, as a special treat, he would hand out wisps of "hundreds and thousands" or chocolate buttons or, best of all, bits of flimsy paper that you stubbed in a corner with a glowing match and waited for a singed worm to wriggle over it till it had outlined a Prince Charming or, if you were unlucky, the words "Beecham's Pills".

Aunt Lil (another of the three sisters) lived, in turn, in Church Road and the Chase. Her cottage in the Chase was opposite a farm where, as at Scotts Farm, you could get a jug of milk for a penny and twenty eggs for a shilling. A short distance away were the Halls — Upper and Nether. The fields here in spring were gold with peggles, and earlier, on Candlemas Day, white with snowdrops. Aunt Lil called the snowdrops "Mary's Tapers". She was like that, Sometimes it was impossible to identify the thing she was speaking about. Sparrows were "Hedge Betties", dragon flies the "devil's knittin'-needles" and the mice, everlastingly in and out of her kitchen, "they skitterin' critters". She was "set" in her ways. She used to boast: "I've never sin a doctor all me life. If me stummick's not gooing ter rights I teks me brimston' an' treacle — but its gotta be stirred wi' a wooden spoon or it won't work." She was a "make-do-and-mend" physician, just as she was a make-do-and-mend surgeon. There was a day when uncle Frank came home with a finger almost severed by a scythe. Aunt Lil rooted about in the cupboard and emerged with a cobweb. She clapped this over the wound, added a dockleaf and bound it all with a strip torn from a freshly-laundered sheet. In three weeks the finger was in one piece and as good as new.

She was a good sort. She had not wanted to leave Church Road for the more inaccessible Chase, but had done so because of a "worritin' " neighbour. The neighbour, she declared, "never 'ad no call ter be born. 'Er gooin's on got me in a fair ol' tizzy, I kin tell yer. When she wer' took to 'er bed an' I went in, friendly-like, ter wet 'er tea an' mend 'er fire, she said she dint want no truck wi' the likes o' me, an' thet if on'y 'er legs 'ad bin wukkin' proper, she'd a sent me abowt me ways. Cunnin' as a cartload o' monkeys thet ol' baggage wer', wi' sovrins under the floor an' no chick nor chil' to spend 'em on." She paused to take breath. "Eat up yer tatters, boy; they ent got no bones in."

Mother often referred to uncle Frank and uncle Fred as "dry old sticks from the same old tree." They were brothers, but they differed. One was content with what he had, the other with what he had not. Uncle Fred was doing well as a hay-merchant and "Brook Lodge" was the beginning of greater and grander things. I was glad for him and for myself. When the place had more or less lost its former identity and grandmother had "released" me for a few weeks, he said, "Yer'll 'ev ter wuk fer yer kip, yer know." And work my my keep I did. I scraped clods of earth from old boots and dressed new ones with neat'sfoot oil or goose-dripping. I chopped the faggots, slashed with a sickle beds of nettles and docks, mucked out the stables, birch-broomed the paths, cleaned the knives and the horse brasses, turned (but only just) the handle of the chaff-cutting machine and, once a week, stood on a stool to help with the harnessing of "Blossom". This was the prelude to adventure, for then aunt Daisy would drive me in the pony-trap to Marden Ash, the other end of Ongar, to sell the brown eggs from her leghorns.

It was a world without tomorrows. After Sunday dinner aunt Daisy would put her feet up on the horsehair sofa and uncle Fred, with a paper and his pipe, would mooch between the rows of sweet peas to the end of the garden where, in the field beyond the stream, he would presently snatch his "forty winks" and where only his God and the walnut-tree would hear his untroubled snores.

On those white and timeless afternoons Ivy (aunt Daisy's and uncle Fred's daughter) and I got out our bikes and rode at random. Sometimes we dismounted at "Moat Farm" and stood like "gapeseeds" at the edge of its sullen pond, poised for speedy flight if anything spooky materialised and floated ghost-like towards us. It was a place of evil; a man had been drowned there. The body had never been found, but every full moon a hand pushed up through the water and brandished an accusing knife. All very King Arthurish. Once we got as far as Matching Green where years ago a Mr. Chimney had established a Marriage Feast Room, but the ride pressed too heavily upon us and we went back to our less arduous itinerary. We often visited aunt Jane, Father's sister, who lived round the corner from "Brook Lodge". She always made us welcome and brought out biscuits and home-made wine almost before she had closed the door behind us.

These journeys apart, we confined our activities to a less strenuous — but much more dangerous — one. Beyond the gate at "Brook Lodge" a hill rose sharply for a hundred yards or so when it fused with the sky. We wheeled our bikes to the top, straddled them and then gusted down it like a couple of demons backed by a gale-force wind to see who could reach the bottom first. Ivy started with an advantage. She had a new machine with a padded and sprung Brooke's saddle, front and back brakes, a free-wheel and pneumatic tyres. I had a rusty old crock that must have gone into the Ark with Noah. There was no padded and sprung Brooke's saddle, no front and back brakes and no free-wheel. Certainly there were no pneumatic tyres, only pock-marked solid ones. Ivy breezed down the hill like the lovely young person she always was; I belted down it like an anthropoid ape, arms rigid, legs stretched out to clear the whizzing pedals and a red-flashing light in the middle of my head gloatingly reminding me that there was always a last time and that this might be it.

Sometimes on those long white afternoons I was lonely; Ivy would have other matters to attend to. I meandered down to the stream, flung a few stones into it and scratched my initials on the crumbling parapet. It was on one of these afternoons that Mrs. Crabbe spoke to me. She had never done so before, always passing me with a dip of her head and a smile that just succeeded in lifting the corners of her mouth. She had been in Ongar the previous day, she said, and had bought a Dean's Rag Book for one of her grandchildren. Would I like to see it? If I approved it her grandchild would aprove it too. I was a little scared of the invitation, but said yes, I did not mind, and walked home with her.

Mrs. Crabbe lived the other side of the "mushroom field" in a white house that almost shook hands with High Laver church. She settled me in a rocking-chair several sizes too big for me and handed me the book. It was a nice book, illustrated in colour and boldly produced. I turned the pages and then gave it back to her. I liked it, I said.

She beamed and told me that I was a sensible little man and that I must come and see her again.

The first time I called she apologised for the door. "Thet's Ben," she smiled, "my 'usband thet was but ent no more. Not a mite o' paint on it from top to bottom. Tent likely there would be, 'im breathin' 'is beer over it fer nigh on twenty years." The second time she apologised for herself. "Kick me if I git under yer fit. I'm thet 'ummocky thet there's no knowin' when I'm standin' up or sittin' down. Not like Ben. If 'e stud be'ind a skewer yer wouldn't a seen 'im." She was unfair to herself. She was big, it is true, but it was a bigness you were unaware of once she had anchored you within her arms and smacked you with a wet-warm kiss. It did not worry her. She ploughed the rough seas of her rustic life like a broadbeamed barge, conscious that the God who in the beginning had made her wanted value for money; but there were Saturday nights when, "sloshin' " in front of the kitchen fire, she mentally chided Him for physical imperfections which, over the years, had kept Ben at arm's length. "It weren't rightly fair." With a lot less here and a lot more there she might have been "as uppish as an 'ollyock an' as pritty as a picksher."

Ben had not been a success as a husband. He drank too much, smoked too much and, except for one passionate night when he seemed to have gone berserk, made love to her hardly at all. And he could not "stay put". He passed swiftly from bird-scaring to milking and from milking to the land, dibbling (so he said) the holes for the wheat. From the first he got cold feet, from the second chapped hands and from the third an absurd little jingle that spun in his head like a top:

"One fer the rook, an' one fer the crow,
One ter die, an' two ter grow."

62

He had been a pig-man at the time of their marriage when, to "git a bit forrader", he took on the job of a shepherd. It was a costly mistake. He did not know that sheep had to be fed to clover bit by bit. He turned his flock into a promising field "an' let 'em eat their 'eads off". The green-stuff fermented inside them and, within days, most of the sheep were dead from bloat. "When 'e come 'ome," Mrs. Crabbe confessed, "'e wer' thet afeared yer could 'ear 'im fer miles. I glouted at 'im an' we 'ad words — as mos' allus we did. I told 'im 'e wer' gormless an' didn't know enough ter git out o' the road of a steamroller. Then I give 'im a mess o' broth an' put 'im ter bed. It dint tek me more'n a month or two ter know I'd mucked me own nest, an' once I got near ter tellin' 'im 'e wernt gooin' ter put 'is fit on me fender never agin. But thet wernt seemly ter my way o' thinkin'. An' mebbe 'twer' me own fault. Come Advent, time I wer' a maid, we used ter pull out a stick from a faggit. If it wer' straight yer 'usband wer' gooin' ter be straight, too. The stick I pulled out wer' straight , but Ben wernt." She sighed. "Me 'ol mum knew better'n me. 'I don't 'old wi' thet man.' she said. "E ent got no git up an' goo.' "

Poor Ben! He swayed from job to job; then, just as he seemed to be settling down "wi' the parish", he died on a snowy Christmas Eve, one hand slopping from his beloved horn mug his wife's elderberry wine and the other crumbling to untasted flakes the first of the twelve mince pies she had set aside for him for twelve happy months. "When 'e wer' took", Mrs. Crabbe recalled, "'e looked like a bit o' knee-sick straw, an' I knew then — when it wer' too late ter tell — thet I'd allus loved 'im, beer an' baccy an' all." Poor Mrs. Crabbe, too! She had done her best to make amends. She went into black for a year, "buried 'im wi' 'am" and pinned a lock of wool against his chest so that Peter would know that on earth he had been a shepherd and, for that reason, had not been "reg'ler ter chuch". "Arter all," he had once surprisingly remarked, "crows don't stop fer no Sundays."

The room I liked best in the house was the kitchen. This was between the "keeping-room" with its stuffed birds and the scullery with the copper that came into its own every Monday "fer the washin' " and every November for the Christmas puddings. It was large and square. Against one of the walls was a white-wood dresser with shelf after shelf of posset-pots, stoneware plates and mugs, and pieces of pewter (cleaned with turnip tops and sand) that winked in the sun but gleamed like shy sentinels when the oil-lamp was lit. Facing the dresser was a brick fireplace with an oak settle, a bacon rack, a pair of wrought-iron cup-dogs and a skillet for mulling wine. On the wall at the side hung a warming-pan and a wimble. "Twer' too 'ome-like fer Ben", commented Mrs. Crabbe. "Time 'e got near a chimbley 'e wernt gooin' out in no cold." Most of the pinewood floor, the knots of which shone like honey-coloured conkers, was taken up by an enormous table. Mrs. Crabbe said it was "the bes' bit o' furnisher fer miles." It was on this table that she made her bread and her cakes and prepared the fruit for her wines and preserves. Here, on "Collop Monday", she cut up all the meat there was in the house and, having dried and salted it, put it away till the end of Lent. Here, too, she compounded her famous Buttercup Salve. Whatever you suffered from, she declared, there was a remedy for it in the hedges and fields — chickweed for boils, ivy-leaves for deafness, nettles for the blood and coltsfoot for Ben's foul pipe. "Yer can't teach Nature nothin' it don't know. All them fancy notions thet some o' they clever young Dicks are gittin' about fertilisers an' such! I'd set me marrers agin anyone's, an' I on'y empty the teapot over 'em an', when I'm minded to, whatever I find in the jakes.

My father, John Charles Smith.
Born Padler's End, Moreton.

My mother, Emily Smith.
Shortly after her "flight" to London,
because she would not recognise
Grandmother's second husband
as her father.

Grandmother Matthews.
Formerly the wife of William Pettit,
blacksmith, Moreton, my
mother's father.

Uncle Walter (in glasses)
with one of his beloved
traction engines.

Scotts Farm, from the orchard, looking towards the village.

MORETON VIEWS

Brook Lodge, Moreton. Home of Uncle Fred and Aunt Daisy. Formerly the "Pig and Whistle".

Village school, Moreton. Only the climbing-frame, the fences and the TV aerial are new.

The blacksmith's, where my mother was born. Now called Forge Cottage. My mother was born in the room behind the top right-hand window. The smithy (now demolished) was sited on the corner where the signpost is.

Jones, of the General Stores, Moreton. Mr Jones in doorway. His son, Harold, is seen right, and Mr Cheek, chief assistant, fourth from left. The tiled roof of the smithy can just be seen, extreme left.

Mr Webster, postmaster, at the door of his shop at Moreton.

The old village pump, Moreton. It used to stand in a yard between the Nag's Head and the school. Now affixed to the wall between school and pub as a reminder of "times past".

Three of the old "sail" reapers.

The Nag's Head
and adjoining house at Moreton.
Photograph by Geoffrey Tyrell.

The 400-year-old
White Hart Inn at Moreton.

Moreton Post Office and Stores.
Photograph by Dennis Shelley.

The Old Vicarage, Moreton
(now a private residence).
Photograph by Ken Whaley.

Thet way they git all the umerous they want."

The "jakes" was the "not-to-be-spoken-about-when-anyone-calls" convenience hidden by the stinging nettles at the far end of the garden. Ben had anticipated by many years the "do-it-yourself" craze and had made it from scraps of wood and roofing-felt conjured from thin air. It was as snug as the saloon-bar into which he often peeped but never entered because of the "extry 'apence". There was a mat that was warm to the feet, and one wall was decorated with a calendar which declaimed over unremembered years:

"Beecham's Pills -
Worth a guinea a box."

Tacked to the inside of the door was a coloured advertisement for Pears Soap. It depicted an unwashed tramp smoking a clay pipe and writing a letter. Beneath it were the words: "Two years ago I used your soap, since when I have used no other."

Sometimes, when the days were short, grandmother arranged with Mrs. Crabbe to let me stay the night with her. They were memorable occasions. Mrs. Crabbe gave me the smaller of the two bedrooms. It smelt of dog-roses and lavender sheets, and a dormer window opened to fields edging green to the rim of the world - the world I had almost forgotten. One day — one day, when I was better, I would have to go back to that world. I pushed that day and that world shamelessly away. I would be sick for a long, long time . . .

Mrs. Crabbe was more than a surprising woman. She walked the four miles to Ongar once a week and returned with groceries and such that would have taxed the strength of any man I knew. "I kin look arter meself, all right", she told me once. And she could. When the tally-

65

man tried to short-change her she marched him by the scruff of his neck to the gate and pitched him across the road into a ditch frothy with meadow-sweet. You would not have thought her superstitious, but she was. There was a juniper-tree at the door to keep the witches away and a bunch of St. John's Wort on the roof to keep the thunder and lightning out. I have no superstitious myself — touch wood! — but I like to remember sharing one with her. It was her birthday. I got up before the pimpernels and sow-thistles were awake and presented her with a newly-picked bunch of may and two unsucked bulls'-eyes. The bulls'-eyes she put on the table; the may she flung into the garden. Then she smacked me, to exorcise, I suppose, the ill-luck I had so unwittingly brought into the house. "Don't never do thet agin!" she flared; "it's suppin' wi' the Devil". The smack did not hurt; the injustice of it did. When she saw the tears in my eyes she suddenly held me close and smothered my mouth with one of her wet-warm kisses. Then she gave me a penny to spend on a sherbet-dab at the Two Miss Prentices.

Dear Mrs. Crabbe! God does not make her sort any more. Perhaps there had been no corner of Heaven big enough to accommodate the mould which once had shaped her dust. Perhaps He had shattered it and, repentant, had pinned against her Essex skies the brilliance of its sturdy stars. The thought would have pleased her. Nobody couldn't 'ave bin no fairer'n thet . . .

CHAPTER EIGHT

There was a game for every month of the year. I do not know by what means the games came; they just did; and in the same ordered sequence as they had come for our fathers before us and for the fathers before theirs. There was no radio, no television and — thank God! no Bingo. Midway between the cottages straggling from the bakery to the church was the Village Hall. This was our cinema, dance-hall and theatre. It was a smallish place, constructed of wood and heated when the nights were cold by one oil-lamp and two "Beatrice" burners. This trinity of warmth was as ineffective as a bundle of grandmother's "dips" would have been, but no one ever suggested replacement. The lamp ("yer've-gotta-pull-it-down-from-the-ceilin'-ter-light-the-blamed-thing") had been the gift of the vicar, and the burners had been fortuitously found in the long grass surrounding a grave in the churchyard. The vicar was proud of the lamp, clicking it down on its chain to trim a wick that was beyond caring every time he entered the place — usually for the purpose of raising funds. The three things made you cough, but no one seemed to mind. I certainly did not; they seemed proper to their environment.

I wonder if we have "progressed" too far and too

quickly? This push-button age is all very nice, but it has obliterated for ever the Romantic Age of the Past. I remember, years later, when gas came to Bethnal Green, how Mother hid the oil-lamp behind a blanket in the kitchen and applied out of sheer enjoyment countless matches to the new and wonderful mantles. The enjoyment was short-lived. There were nights when, after we had seen 'Maria Marten" or "Sweeney Todd" at the Forester's Music Hall in Cambridge Heath Road, Father would stand at the dark entrance to a dark room to strike a match before wending an uncertain way to where he thought the gas-mantle was. His judgment was often faulty. The gas-mantle was usually to all points east or all points west. Mother "shushed" him when he swore and counselled him that if only he moved right a bit, or left a bit, he would be on target. It was not long before the blanket was removed from the bump in the kitchen and the lamp restored over the ring still visible on its former resting place.

Much of the "boredom" of today's youngsters stems, I think, from an absence of contrast. They were born in a world where everything was waiting for them on a plate. There has been no transition of values. Their "old-fashioned" mums and dads had to create their own enjoyment, sitting down at a fretted piano and stroking out:

"Kathleen Mavourneen! the grey dawn is breaking,"

or grinding a gramophone handle for one wheezy tune. Even going to church was work of a sort. There was all that preparation. No jeans, no open-neck shirts, but the dressing up in a Sunday-best suit and the singing of psalms that went up when you went down and down when you went up. I hesitate to plead in defence of sermons, for then they were timed by hour-glass or watch and were hard for that part of the body you sat on. But at least they made you think and, perhaps, shaped you for the week ahead. And then there were books. Most of these were forbidding and pointed a moral, but there was nothing wrong with Marryat's "Mr. Midshipman Easy" or Kingsley's "The Water Babies". Mother did her best to get me to read "Uncle Tom's Cabin" and grandmother, when she had tucked me up, would leave "Pilgrim's Progress" by the side of the bed. She had never read it herself but had heard that it was a "good" book which might "make summat" of me. My Father had the right idea. He would bring home "Comic Cuts" and "Chips" and throw them on the table. "Leave the boy be," he would say to Mother, "'e'll find 'is own level when he wants ter."

As I have said, the games came. They were there, in the roads, in the fields, even in the "Nag's Head" yard, where the pump afforded a right of sanctuary as inviolable as that of the churches of Anglo-Saxon England. The only ones outside this ordered list were those like Knocking Down Ginger, when we rat-tatted at doors and streaked like the mad things we were into a wrapped-up night, and Mind the Thread, Lady. In this, two boys sat opposite each other, supposingly holding the ends of a length of cotton over which the victim (usually an old woman) uneasily stepped, lifting as she did so voluminous skirts.

January, being cold, was the time for Tig (or Touch), a variation of this being Tom Tiddler's Ground. Then there was King of the Castle:

"I'm the king of the castle,
Get down you dirty rascal."

This, a rarin'-to-go game, was usually played by the boys.

69

A similar one was Roman Soldiers, where two rows of boys faced each other and shouted:

"Bang! bang! bang!
Are you ready for a fight?
We are the Roman Soldiers."

It seldom ended without a free-for-all, often severely suppressed by Mr. Gordon, the headmaster, or by Mr. Ball, the baker.

February was the month for ball and stone games: Rounders, Ball in the Cap, Tip and Run and Fivestones. Fivestones was reputed to be one of the oldest games in the world and a successor to Knucklebones and Jackstones, when it was played to the singing rhyme:

"Nick nack, Paddy Whack,
Give a dog a bone
This old man came rolling home.
This old man
He played one,
He played Nick nack on my drum.
Nick nack Paddy Whack,
Give a dog a bone,
This old man came rolling home."

It was a girls' game. They sat or knelt and tossed up what they called a "gob", catching it as it came down and scooping up with the same hand one, two, three and then four other gobs lying on the ground. It was a game that called for a certain amount of dexterity that we boys knew we could never emulate.

March was peg-top month, when last-year's favourites were unwrapped and oiled or new ones bought. There were three types of peg-tops: the peg-top proper, the racer and the boxer. Moreton's flinty roads afforded little scope for the last two (the boxer was a "cissy", anyway), but the peg-top proper could be used with equal facility here and in the asphalted playground of the school. It had a large, pear-shaped body and a vicious looking steel spike which, when accurately aimed, could splinter another in two. A "counting-out" rhyme went with the game:

"Eena, meena, mina, moe,
Catch a nigger by his toe;
If he hollers let him go,
Eena, meena, mina, moe.
O-U-T spells out!"

The boy with whom the rhyming stopped was unlucky. The spike of his top was plunged into the ground so that the top stood upright. The other boys formed a circle and then aimed at it in turn. The result was always the same, and sixpence earned for a week's bird-scaring was lost before the formation and trickle of the first tear. It was a cruel game.

Hopscotch was "girls-only", and this, too, was played within the school railings, where the lines could be properly "scotched" with chalk. Stones and bits of glass from ginger-beer bottles were mostly used for the "pick", but now and again some of the girls produced a gailycoloured piece of china called a "chaney". Chaneys were highly prized and carried in pinafore pockets as proudly as the gold sovereigns on gold Alberts were carried to Sunday church by the top-hatted gentry.

A favourite game was The King's Horses. One of the boys stood against the wall while others made "backs", each hanging on to the coat-tails in front. The rest made a running jump and leaped as far as they could along the backs of the "horses" until, with the ever-increasing weight, they gave way. I mention this game because, although it was often played, I never understood the words which accompanied it. They went, as far as I can phonetically recall:

> "Old Jimmy Knack-o, one, two, three,
> Old Bob Bee, Old Bob Bee,
> And AWAY!"

With the coming of April, that proud-pied month, the fierce energies of winter wilted and games became more respectable and less turbulent. There were not many; indeed, I can recall only two: See-Sawing and Skipping. Both boys and girls shared in the first, but the girls, to whom the second rightfully belonged, were always glad to enlist the boys' help, if only for turning the ropes. There were many games within the game: Salt, Mustard, Vinegar, Pepper (the best-known, I suppose), Double Dutch, Visiting, Begging, Chasing the Fox and Rocking the Cradle. A feature of them all, as with other games, was the rhyming verse. One I remember well:

> "I see the moon and the moon sees me,
> God bless the moon and God bless me;
> Grace in the garden, grace in the hall,
> And the grace of God be on us all."

See-sawing, too, had its rhyme:

> "See-saw, Margery Daw,
> Johnnie shall have a new master.
> He will have but a penny a day
> Because he can't go any faster."

May, June and July were loved because of their Singing

72

and Ring Games: Nuts in May (nuts being a corruption of "knots", a posy of flowers), Poor Mary Sits A-weeping, Kiss-in-the-Ring (always good for a full muster of boys!), London Bridge is Broken Down, Oranges and Lemons, and many, many more.

August and September, when "light thickens, and the crow makes wing to the rooky woods", were not particularly happy months for games. Most of them, like Green Gravel and Who Killed Cock Robin? skirted the perimeter of something we did not understand and did not want to understand; the end of anything was always afar off. Besides, tomorrow would be October and Marbles: "blood-alleys" and "glasseys" and "taws"; and Buttons: "sinkeys" and "shankeys" and "two-ers" and "three-ers". Best of all there would be Kites, paper shapes with paper tails that an unsuspecting mum had left as curlers over a wash-'us sink. And October was the month of Hallowe'en, when witches on sheep-trays went galloping by, and gouged-out turnips, with candles for eyes, were shamelessly employed to "frit" in the dark the unwary.

November was the month for Hoops and Indoor Games. The hoops, iron things as tall as we were, were bowled along the narrow roads with skimmers shaped like a shepherd's crook. The games we played around a faggot fire within an ever-decreasing circle of lamp-light, games with pencil and paper, games with string and, sometimes, when uncles and aunts were away at the village hall, games with the cards used by them for Banker at Christmas. Christmas! December! That was the time we counted our pennies and bought presents we could ill afford, played "Here we go round the mulberry bush" and sang as much as we could remember of "The Twelve Days -". It was a tidying-up month when toys and memories of things past were over-shadowed by trees, stockings, carol-singers and an unremarked feeling of one-ness.

The child, unlike the man, is immortal. He will play his games and sing his songs till, as my Father used to say, "the cows stop comin' 'ome". When the last shadow of the last evening steals across the last sky I would rather hear the familiar voices of children singing on an Essex green than the unfamiliar ones of angels and archangels and all that blessed company of the apostles hallooing in Heaven sabbatical psalms.

CHAPTER NINE

I never knew Grannie Smith, my Father's mother, although I have often been reminded that, when she got the chance, she jigged me up and down and cooed, "Is 'e 'is Gran's ickle dumplin', then!" It was a mercy that the good Lord withheld from her the gift of foresight. I shudder to think what her reaction would have been had she known that one day her ickle dumpling would be an ickle rude sailor in a big rude Navy.

I suppose there must be something in heredity. There are times when I am chasing aunt Maude's "right word in the right place, Charles dear," when I stop to wonder where the urge for the self-infliction of pain comes from. I know of one source. Owd Grannie Smith. It is no matter for surprise that she kept what then was known as a "Commonplace Book". What is surprising is that most of the pages of that Commonplace Book were devoted to poetry and prose. Father knew of it. It had been on the whatnot in the only-for-Sundays room all his unmarried life, but only when gran was lying so strangely still under the thatched roof of her cottage at Padler's End did he take the key from her neck and snap back for the first time its big brass lock. Years later he snapped back the lock again, this time under the roof of an air-raid shelter. We looked at it together through the loud hours of a seemingly endless night; then, like a modern Sir Philip Sidney, he pressed the scuffed volume into my hands. "You tek it, boy," he said; "you need it more'n I do."

As well as poetry and prose the book was a miscellany of odds and ends, all in the honest-to-goodness script of a country child. There were recipes for wine and food; cures for whooping cough and housemaid's knee; old wives' tales and superstitions; beauty, household and first-aid hints, and the chit-chat of local gossip. There were, too, as well as extracts from many of the near-indecipherable letters penned by grandfather to grandmother, cuttings from newspapers and periodicals. There was this, for instance (from the Ladies' Treasury, 1858) which intrigued me as much as it must have intrigued the reader all those Victorian years ago: "Has he any call to be a husband who kisses his wife only on Saturday night? Who leaves his wife to blow out the lamp and bruise her precious little toes while she is navigating for the bedpost?" And this (from the Lady's Magazine, 1828): "My daughters are living instances of the baneful consequences of the dreadful fashion of squeezing the waist until the body resembles that of an ant. Their stays are bound with iron in the holes through which the laces are drawn so as to bear the tremendous tugging which is intended to reduce so important a part of the human frame to a third of its natural proportion. They are unable to stand, sit, or walk as women used to do. To expect one of them to stoop would be absurd. My daughter Margaret made the experiment the other day: her stays gave way with a tremendous explosion, and down she fell upon the ground, and I thought she had snapped in two."

Grandmother had obviously been a great humourist.

She must have been a great lover too. Had she, I wondered, been thinking of grandfather when she copied in its entirety Elizabeth Barrett Browning's:

"How do I love thee? Let me count the ways.
I love thee to the depth and breadth and height
My soul can reach . . ." ?

or when she wrote:

"A youth to whom was given
So much of earth, so much of heaven." ?

Certainly he must have been in her mind when (I imagine) he died, for halfway through the book, in coloured ink, was this: "At one stride came the dark," bolstered by Byron's:
". . . He had kept
The whiteness of his soul,
And thus men o'er him wept."

If I interpret aright grandmother must have taken grandfather's death badly, for following that was Emerson's: "There is a crack in everything God has made." This was a confession of shaken faith which must have shamed her, for after it came: "I will lift up mine eyes unto the hills, from whence cometh my help." Even that, it appeared, was not contrition enough, for it was supplemented by a defiant: "I will be conquered; I will not capitulate." I can see her now, four-square to all the winds that ever blew, dashing the tears from her mutinous eyes and thundering: "What goes for Doctor Johnson goes for me, too."

Hereabouts there creeps into the book a vein of philosophy which sallies along to the end. It is heralded by Abraham Lincoln's: "The struggle for today is not altogether for today. It is for a vast future also." A jump or two ahead and there are three more entries, lumped together like this:

"And if I laugh at any mortal thing
'Tis that I may not weep."

"In the hum of the market place there
is money, but under the cherry-tree there
is rest."

"The hours when the mind is absorbed by
beauty are the only hours when we really
live."

What impressed me more than anything else was grandmother's love of the written word. My Father never thought of himself as anything other than a product of the soil from which he and his forbears had sprung, and it is reasonable to assume that grandmother thought of herself in the same way. Her education had been nothing to write home about and her social background had been that of a back-o'-beyond village which she had never left and had never wanted to leave. The pedlar came to her door with his bits and pieces; the rest she got from Moreton, over the bridge, or once a week from Ongar, three miles away. Whence then had stemmed her learning? Father thought he knew. "Books," he said. "She was allus readin'. She jes' found the words an' wrote 'em down." It was a convenient explanation which we did not pursue. Bombs permitting, there was always tomorrow.

"She jes' found the words — " "Jewels ... that on the outstretched finger of time sparkle for ever." Her tongue must have proudly protruded when she wrote this, by

Keats: "Here are sweet peas, on tip-toe for a flight;" or this, by James Thomson: " . . . And villages embosomed soft in trees;" or this, by Andrew Marvell:

" . . . Orange bright,
Like golden lamps in a green night."

And I know without a shadow of doubt that when she had primly blotted Tennyson's: "Laburnums, dropping wells of fire," and Shakespeare's: ". . . The white wonder of Juliet's hand," she must have straightened her back against the antimacassar on the horsehair chair and breathed with God, "It is good!"

I wish I had known Owd Grannie Smith; she must have been a great Englishwoman, with a smell in her native earth better than all the perfumes of the East. One of her last thoughts as she lay dying in that cluttered little room was surely of sunshine freckling a country lane. The gods sometimes nod. She should have been a Hawkins, a Raleigh, a Drake. She should have thundered to glory with, on her lips: "I have taken the depth of the water, and when my vessel sinks my flag will still fly." Perhaps she had been born out of time. There might have been a niche for her somewhere in World War II. If so, there might then have been no bombing. With her arms akimbo and her face upturned to an English sky the "Luftwaffe" would not have *dared* . . .

CHAPTER TEN

When the Navy had done with me at the end of World War I my Commanding Officer, who for years had threatened me with "King's Rules and Regulations", pointedly wrote in my Rupert Brooke: "Memory is the thing you forgot with". I do not deny I deserved it; I had forgotten so many things. I still do forget so many things. In the garden the other day, where I had one eye on the bulbs that were to come before the swallow dared, and the other on the cat on the roof of the shed, the word "huffer" swam out of the blue and perched like a wrinkled imp on the tip of my dibber. I had forgotten that, too, though in 1904 my cousins and I had bought huffers (rolls of newly-baked bread) by the dozen from Mr. Ball. Memory is like that with me. I can try for hours to recall the name of the man who, Sunday after Sunday, nods with me under the pulpit; then, just as I am wondering whether I bolted the door or put out that note for tomorrow's extra pinta, it stabs at me with the speed of light.

I know someone who, unless he is able to flip-flop his hands like a Greek, is as speechless as a mute. It is not hands with me, but pen and paper. The words that have slept for unremembered years suddenly rub their eyes and drip to the point of my pen almost before I am ready to give them shape. There are two there now: "flummergasted" (astonished) and "blatherskite" (a boastful person). I owe them both to Bob Britton, one of my uncle Fred's men, who insisted that the English he spoke was no "curiouser" than that spoken by "they arsy-varsy furriners as dint 'ev no proper know." I reminded him once that I was a cockney and a "furriner", too, but he brotherly brushed that aside. "I don't tek no count o'thet, boy," he said. "Taint likely. Yer never wanted yer should be born in Lunnon, did yer?" Not only that. My Mother was a Moreton woman and my Father a Padler's End man, both of which qualifications gave me an unassailable title to the Essex that had been, the Essex that was, and the Essex that was likely to be.

In contrast to Bob, who was short and fat, the other of uncle Fred's men, Andy, was as lean and hungry-looking as Shakespeare's Cassius. Andy was mild and inoffensive, but quick to anger. Around the corner from Brook Lodge was Beehive Cottage, an attractive thatched place let every June to a man and his wife who dolled themselves up and blustered on hired hacks into every sacrosanct corner of the village. One day they clattered past the gate where Andy, a straw between his teeth, was "tekkin' a breather". The man looked at Andy and then at his wife. "The fellow I was telling you about, my dear," he said — "the perfect Essex bumpkin." Andy went white, stood still for a moment or two and then went indoors. He returned with the coach-horn that uncle Fred kept over the mantelpiece in the parlour and leaned over the gate again. "Reckon as 'ow they gormless critters'll be back afore long", he said grimly. He was right. They came down the hill in a smother of dust and breasted the gate. It was Andy's moment of revenge. He levelled the horn across the road till it almost touched the leading horse's ear and blew an almighty blast that would have made old Triton's shell sound like a toy trumpet. The horse whinnied like mad and threw its rider — the man. Andy shambled over to him and said quietly, "It wernt seemly ter call me thet, mister. Do yer do it agin an' I'll set yer ter rights wi' me gun. Now up on yer fit an' git. I mun dutty me 'ands on nobody's washin' no more." He handed the horn to uncle Fred, who had witnessed the incident. "I ent no bum'kin, boss," he said. "Me mother ped penny a wik fer me learnin' an' I kin rid ev'ry wud in the Bible — "ceptin'," he added thoughtfully, "them 'ard uns in Gen'sis 'leven."

Uncle Fred was "broad" himself, but he was making headway as a hay-merchant and meeting business associates whose social status was different from his own. The broadness was battered but not bent. Aunt Daisy told him he was making a fool of himself, putting "haitches" where they were not wanted and leaving them out where they were, and twitted him with, "'Ave yer 'ung up yer 'at on the 'ook in the 'all?" when he clumped into the house in "barmed-up" boots. An unexpected visit to France did nothing to ease things. He came back with *bureau de poste* for the shop in the village where Mr. Webster sold stamps, and *coupez-les seulement derriere la tete et les orielles* for Fred Marrable when he called on Sundays to give him a short back-and-sides.

Much of the dialect pushed by over-zealous writers into the mouths of the Essex men and women of my day is phoney. It is so easy to distort a word so that it "looks Essex". My corner of the county was small, I know, but I never heard "storve" for starve, "porch" for poach, or "charmber" for chamber. (This last, in fact, was called something that neither looked like "chamber" nor sounded like it — and was "not quite nice.") Words I am doubtful about are words like "bettermost" (better than), "enquiration" (enquiry), "crossquabble" (to question), and "spinnick" (a fretful child). But of "trinkle" for trickle I have no doubts whatsoever. It might have been all right for Chaucer in the fourteenth century, but not for the villagers of Moreton early in the twentieth.

The things I liked the "mostest" (legitimate!) were not the parts of speech, but the simple honest-to-goodness sentences. These wove their melodic strands into primitive patterns of sound that no Elgar or Holst could have dreamed up in a thousand musical years. How many Fowlers would it have taken to fashion this: "She ent gotta thought above 'er stummick"? Or: "He kep on 'ummin' an' 'awin' like 'e wer' standin' fer Judgement Day"? Or: "She wer' a cunnin' owd cup o' tea"?

After my first stupefying visit to the English Lakes, I asked a geologist friend how it had all happened. He said:

" 'First it rained and then it blew,
Then it frizzed and then it snew;
Then it rained and blew again,
Then it frizzed and snew again.'

But, seriously . . . Millions of years ago, when all those volcanoes got going —" He grinned sheepishly and reached down a Bible from the shelf behind him. "This says it better than I can." He read: " 'And God said, let the waters under the heaven be gathered into one place and let the dry land appear.' " He closed the book and put it back. "That answer your question?" I told him it did. Now, at a much later date, it answers another: How had the Essex dialect happened? I know the stock reply: Britain's invading hordes — the Romans, the Picts, the Scots, the Angles, the Saxons ("the men of the long knives"), the Danes and the Normans under William. But is it the real reply? All those dishevelled years ago Andy

83

had said, "I kin rid ev'ry wud in the Bible." So can I, but I am content with a few. "And God called the dry land earth" ... Might he not also have called the crude beginnings of speech over one small part of that earth the "Essex Dialect"? And might not that have been an additional reason for the words "And God saw that it was good" my geologist friend omitted from his quotation? I like to think so. There was nothing original in Listz's "Give me a laundry list and I will set it to music." God had said it aeons ago. But it had not been a laundry list; it had been the Essex dialect.

CHAPTER ELEVEN

Andy, the senior of uncle Fred's men, had once boasted: "I kin rid ev'ry wud in the Bible." I do not think he would have been able to "rid" the words in Bob's, his mate's, scrawled as they were inside the cover of the only book he had perhaps ever possessed — the Bible. They were blotted and blotched and torn apart and slithered, almost illegible, down to the bottom right-hand corner:

> "Black is the raven,
> Black is the rook,
> But blacker the sinner
> That pinches this book."

Aunt Daisy "tuk 'er solemn oath" that once Bob had told her that her teeth were like a flock of sheep that had come up from the washing. No one believed her. Bob had no more poetry in him than the chaff he cut every day or the hay he carted to Aldgate every week. All the same, there must have been within him those "immortal longings" of the bard. When he died aunt Daisy found the Bible snug in the corner of a cotton bag. A celluloid cross and a musty Sunday School card for "diligence and good attendance" protruded from the "Song of Solomon".

She ran down the stairs and thrust the Bible at uncle Fred. "I allus told yer so," she said, "now see fer yerself. Chapter 4, verse 2. 'Thy teeth are like a flock of sheep—'". Uncle Fred read the lines — and more. "Um!" he said, and chuckled, "Yer wouldn't a bin so 'igh an' mighty if it 'ad bin verse 5, would yer?"

No, Bob was no poet; nor would he ever be. Nevertheless, he caressed the things of an Essex earth as a young Kreisler was then caressing the strings of a violin. I recall a morning when mists were probing with thin fingers unprotesting hedges. Bob was pruning a pear-tree in the hoppet. "Nuthin' like pear fer scentin' a room", he said. "Or cherry an' apple. Ash is better fer burnin', though. Chestnut's n' good. 'Olly neither — less yer uses it green. Melts like a candle. An' birch don't last. Oak's the best, but it's gotta be old an' dry. Then it'll 'eat yer innards like a tot o' Nelson's blood."

He had an uncanny knack of finding mushrooms where no one else thought of looking for them. "But," he warned, "mushrooms is queer." There were the "right 'uns" and the "wrong 'uns". The right ones ("puff-balls", he called them) had purple spores and pinkish gills; they had to be picked young. The wrong ones, sometimes as big as pumpkins, were as tough as old boots. You could cut them up with a sharp knife and use them to strop your razor with.

No one knew whether it was true or not, but Bob swore that he had been with Lovat's Scouts in the Boer War. He could "read" a trail more fluently than I could read the School Board for London primer left behind in London. The hind hoof of a walking horse would be in front of the fore, and it would be longer and narrower. The same horse, galloping, would leave a line of isolated hoof-marks, the greater the distance between them indicating the speed at which it was being driven. So with the pad-marks of a fox, or the straggling ones of a dog. Hobnails revealed the farmer or, perhaps, the gamekeeper, while the "toes-turned-in" in the spinney meant that "'angmouth Joe from 'Igh Laver 'as bin arter they pheasants agin. Though thet don't signify," Bob reflected. "Come the full moon 'e's as daft as a shillin's-wuth o' fardens. Does mos' of 'is poachin' out o' the breedin' season, when the birds lay up in the fields. When they're disturbed they kuk-kuk like mad an' wake the dead in the chu'chyard."

I never knew him not to be able to identify a plant or a flower. To "'is way o' thinkin" the ugliest was "Come-you-home-husband-though-never-so-drunk" for the yellow stonecrop and, the prettiest, "Traveller's Joy" for the clematis. Between these there was "Lords and Ladies" for the cuckoo-pint, "Old Man's Nightcap" for the wild convolvulus, "Plum Pudding" for the red campion, "Sons before Fathers" for the coltsfoot, and "Shirt Buttons" for the greater stitchwort. The plant I liked best was one of the docks. Its long stems were festooned with brown seeds the size of a withered pea. These we called "tea-leaves", and ran fingers and thumb up their stem for handfuls to throw over each other at school. There was a barrel of rue tea at the door of "Brook Lodge", and Andy and he were required by uncle Fred to take a mugful before every meal. Next to rue Bob believed that there was nothing like nettles for the blood. "The on'y thing wrong wi' they," he said, "is they sting. An' they don't do thet if yer knows 'ow t'andle 'em." Which reminded me of the verse:

"Tender-fingered grasp a nettle,
And it stings you for your pains;
Grasp it like a man of mettle,
And it soft as silk remains."

As with plants, so with birds. "'Ark!" he'd say all at once, "the yellow'ammer. A-little-bit-o'-bread-an'-cheese." Or: "'ear thet? The love-cry o' the plover. Spring ent far away now." He had little time for starlings; they were seldom themselves, borrowing other birds' songs and passing them off as their own. And they were "so tarnation noisy", everlastingly clicking their castanets and beating their little drums. The robin and the wren, now ... they were different.

> "The robin-redbreast and the wren
> Be God Almighty's cock and hen,"

and if either suffered a broken leg by being caught in a trap, God Almighty saw to it that the trapper suffered one, too.

Apart from that long journey to South Africa and the shorter ones to Aldgate, Bob had never left the Essex he had been born in. There was no reason why he should have done. His roots were as deep in its soil as the roots of "they gret ol' trees" which, only a stone's throw from the loft he slept in, doffed him their morning caps. There was another reason. His mother lived "way over Fyfield" and once a week he walked the three country miles to see her. She was a sprightly old lady, with apple-red cheeks as smooth as his own, who "cried like a bebby" when the "Old Queen" died because, early in life she had lost her "dear Albert" and because she had been responsible for bringing down the price of the quartern loaf. She still "ridded-up" and hearth-stoned an antiquated fireplace, still wore pattens to keep her feet clear of mud, and still wore for Sunday church a black tippet pinned at the front with nasturtiums. Her cottage was small, but big enough for present need, with a chintz-covered bed lined up with the floor-boards. Away at the back was the "muck'll", where the earch-closet was emptied and into which the pigsty drained. There were still two pigs. It had been one of Bob's jobs to feed their sires. He mashed up "taters" and mixed them with everything he could lay his hands on: snails from the morning's wet hedges, dandelions, nettles, thistles and grass from the fertile fields. "An' a right ol' mess it wer", he confessed, grinning from ear to ear, "but it made lovely 'am an' chitluns thet melted in yer mouth soon as yer looked at 'em."

His religion was simple and direct: belief in a God who gave him his daily bread and a creed that bade him to order himself lowly and reverently before his betters. He went to church as a boy, sang in the choir (his favourite hymn was "There is a green hill far away"), sketched in the prayer-books "likenesses" of the flibbertigibbets he had gone gallivanting with over at the sandpits, and pumped air for the organ. He also carved his name on the back of one of the varnished pews for which, as the "ol' pusson" was one of the school governors, he received the cane on each hand. "Still," he said, "it dint ut. I rubbed me 'ands wi' an onion fust."

Every night he pulled on an old "gunsey" and ambled down to the "White Hart" for a tankard of half-and-half. Belloc was thirty-something then, but Bob had never heard of him. If he had and had read him he would have endorsed to the hilt his "When you have lost your inns, drown your empty selves, for you will have lost the last of England." Since 1896, when the speed-limit had been raised from four to fourteen miles an hour, motorists with their "arf-crown words" had been trickling into the "White Hart" and the "Nag's Head" in ever-increasing numbers, and the places were not the same. He supposed it was because of that "Progress" which nowadays seemed to be lapping against everyone's lips. There were times when, to assuage a nascent gloom and "ter stay me

89

stummick", he gulped down one for the road and sang
"White Wings" all the dark way home:

"White wings they never grow weary,
They carry me over the bright summer sea,
White wings they never grow weary,
I'll spread out my white wings and sail home
    to thee."

He had a plummy sort of voice which you felt could be
squeezed between fingers and thumb till the juices ran. It
was not everyone's kind of music, but it was good enough
for him.

Bob had never married. Perhaps that is why he loved
children so much. Perhaps that is why they loved him.
Sometimes, when there was no school, they came to
"Brook Lodge" in a bunch, imploring him to set them to
work. He gave each of them a sweet and told them to "git
on polishin' them 'oss-brasses", or replenishing the oil in
the carriage-lamps or, if they were not in their best
clothes, washing the mud from the hay-wagon's wheels.
Aunt Daisy plied them with lemonade when they had
done and urged them to be off home. She knew Bob. He
would settle the children in a ring and show them how to
make bows and arrows from hazel wands, or reins from a
skein of wool, a cotton-reel and four shortened pins or,
even, corn-dollies from the best of the wheat. He showed
them (but did not let them touch) the silver watch left him
by his father. It did not go now. The son managed to do
what the father had feared to do if he wound it — break
the spring. And that within an hour of the old man's
death. His mother said it was a "sign" and that the watch
should be disposed of. Bob agreed that it was a sign, all
right — a sign that it should have been wound "reg'lar
like" — but refused to throw it away. He made a

"shammie" bag for it and clipped it to the end of a chain the thickness of a hawser. It still told the time. The hands had stopped at twelve, but whenever the sun was immediately over his head he eased it gently out of the bag and stared at it as, centuries ago, he might have stared at a babe in a Bethlehem crib. What could not speak could not lie. It was "allus dead right".

****

He died in the morning of an April day, when charlock was stabbing the oat-fields with gold and, down in the village, flowering currants were peeping red-eyed into other people's gardens. He would not have questioned his passing. He had run the straight race; he had fought the good fight and, with Hudson, had loved the birds and the green places and the wind on the heath. And, man and boy, he had known the brightness of the skirts of God. All that, at ninety, "wer' summat ter be thenkful fer."

CHAPTER TWELVE

At this time uncle Walter, one of Mother's step-brothers, was starting a traction-engine business which in the next few years was to make him one of the most important men in Moreton. He lived in one of the Corner Houses where the road right-turned to the mill, and had built in the field behind it a workshop as seductive in its way as the forge. I spent many happy hours there. He showed me how to shape wood on the lathe and how to put a cutting-edge on a chisel. The grindstone was a cumbersome one, two feet or so across and rotated by a rusty handle in a rusty clamp. I could not turn and grind at the same time, so uncle Walter fixed up a vice that gripped the chisel and angled it correctly against the stone. It was demanding work which, more often than not, left my hands blistered for days. The blisters did not worry uncle Walter. "If thet's all yer git on 'em when yer come a man," he said, "yer won't ev nuthin' to fret about."

I liked uncle Walter. For some reason I never knew he called me "Cap'n" and fired at me from time to time questions like "Where does the wind go when it stops?" and "Ow long is a piece of string?" When I posed them to grandmother she said, "Oh, thet boy! When *will* 'e grow up?" He hired out his one engine to farmers for heavy work and threshing. Sometimes, when it was sniff-snuffing over the gritty road, he would bring it to a complaining halt and shout, "Like a ride, Cap'n?" It was an invitation I never refused. I climbed the emery-papered steps and eased myself into a cab as remote from reality as the cockpit of a "Spitfire", a cab of pistons and smells and grease and a fly-wheel that spun so fast that you never knew when it had stopped. Often, when there was no school, he took me along to the threshings. Then a belt was fitted to the wheel so that it could power the elevator which carried the spent straw from the threshing drum to the hopper and, finally, to the chaff-box, where it was chopped up. I was never allowed to be idle on these occasions. Someone would press a wimble into my hands and tell me to turn. Then the wimble would be fed with lengths of straw which, inch by inch as I turned, became a rope. This was then looped over stakes driven into the ground to stop it curling and, when it was required, used for trussing.

Little by little Essex was giving birth to a dimension which became me as naturally as a shell becomes a snail. The fine tendrils of boyish perception reached out and caught at their tips a new world of sight and sound and smell which was to lie in wait for the riper years. When in that rainless summer the harvest came I was out in the fields from dawn till dusk. Grandfather and his men did the work, but grandmother saw to their "innards". She was up at cock-crow, plugging the scooped-out tops of her home-made loaves with butter the colour of gold and carving great chunks of glowing cheese, which she sand-wiched to keep fresh between dock-leaves newly pulled from the drowsy hedge. And, after all that, the beer, a gallon for each man in earthenware bottles I could just about manage to lift. "Cuttin' corn's thusty wuk, boy. The men'll need thet an' more. They gotta make up their sweat.

Cutting corn *was* thirsty work. Two men with scythes went round the edges of the field making swathes for the reaper. Scything was not the easy thing it seemed. If you swung clumsily and without rhythm you could stab the point of your blade into the ground and gash your shins to the bone. Rhythm was the whole secret. The men stood with the left foot a little behind the right, their hands gripping the nibs of the shead (long handle). The stroke was started with the right hand to the front of the right knee, the hand then moving smartly towards the left knee. There was never a sense of haste, the sustained oiled swing controlled as it was to a shining inch by the gnarled hands of craftsmen in love with their work.

The scythers were followed by the reaper. This bent the wheat to the cutting knife and shuttled it out to the women behind, who bound it into sheaves. It was superseded by the combined reaper and binder — which was not without its drawbacks. The twine often broke and it had to be stopped for repairs. The women liked it better. Binding by hand had been a painful business, lacerating hands and arms almost beyond belief.

When the break came for "elevenses" everyone sought the shade of a hedge, cool after the hot sun, but where "them blamed wopses" zoomed in defence. Most of the men brought their own food, but the wives and children of those who lived near brought it to the field in linen "wittal pokes". It was an animated break, which I understood without understanding. Songs were sung and earthy tales went their primitive rounds. One of my aunts sang, sweetly, I recall, but with monotonous repetition, all ten verses of "A frog he would a-wooing ride, ah hoo, ah hoo", and Tubby, the cowman, with a voice like a wounded nail, told the story of Lady Nancy Bell who died while her sweetheart, Lord Lovell, was absent in a "far countrie" who, when he returned and learnt of the lovely Nancy's death, died too, broken by grief.

"And they buried her in the chancel high,
And they buried him in the choir;
And out of her grave sprang a red, red rose,
And out of his sprang a briar."

For me, and for most of the villagers, the exciting part of the harvest came when the corn was reduced to a small area in the middle of the field. Here, driven into it by the gradual encroachment of the reaper, the rabbits hid themselves. When, finally, it was too small for further concealment, they made a frantic dash for freedom. Often it was too late. Men — and women, too — armed with guns and sticks, shot them or clubbed them to death. It was a sad end for the vanquished, but a happy one for the victors. Rabbit pie was on the menu of most of the cottagers for weeks afterwards.

When the corn had been harvested and dried it was pitchforked into painted wagons and carted away. The church bells were rung, the horses were decorated with rosettes and ribbons, and those children lucky enough to have been chosen sat astride them for the journey back to the farm. It was not an easy matter for young legs to straddle the broad back of a shaft-horse but oh! how it was worth it. It was so wonderful. There we were, "up above the world so high", the sword of make-believe in our hands and the cap of courage on our heads, monarchs of all we surveyed. A simple pleasure, I suppose, compared with the pleasures of today, but one, I dare swear, completer and more enduring.

There may have been gleaning (or "leazing" as it was sometimes called) in those days, but I cannot remember it. There was when my Mother was a girl. The women gathered outside the gate and waited for the "gleaning bell". When this sounded they rushed the field with their sacks and filled them with corn left by the reaper. This they took to the miller, who either charged them for grinding it or took a percentage of the flour for his own use. A good night's work would see most of the villagers through the winter. Small wonder they baked their own bread!

Bob Britton had his Song of Solomon. I have my Genesis. "While the earth remaineth, seed time and harvest, and cold and heat, and summer and winter, and day and night shall not cease."

Seed time and harvest ... Comforting words, are they not?

CHAPTER THIRTEEN

I referred earlier to the scythers as "craftsmen". Perhaps the word should have been "artists". Craftsmen proper were the smiths, the thatchers, the wheelwrights, the saddle, hurdle, and basket-makers. But, artists or craftsmen, it is all the same. Their work has either gone for good or, where it still survives, is but a pale shadow of its former self. The specialist, the man who could start and finish a job with his own two hands and stand back and say "This is mine! — I made it!" has been murdered by the machine. There is no dirtier hyphenated word in the English language than "production-line".

In those days there was not the controversy about hedges that there is now. There was a belief here and there among the arable farmers that they took from the soil much of its fertility and harboured birds and vermin that were "never n' good ter man n' beast". The stock farmer, however, was in favour of them; they sheltered his cattle and sheep, acted as windbreaks, and defined his boundaries. They were costly to maintain, but once they were "laid" they were good for years.

Grandfather, at Scotts Farm, gave as little thought to hedges as he did to white ties and tails, but beyond the signpost, along the road that led to the Roothings, a hedger-and-ditcher was employed all the year round. The man often flung me a smile and a bright "good-day!" and once, when a frisky nor'-easter was whipping the morning to wrath, beckoned me over the gate to share with him his fire and his fat-pork roll. He draped a sack over my shoulders and sat me on another. "My!" he said, "ye be cold, boy! An' no wunner! Know what the det is?" I shook my head. "Thirtinth January. Feast o' St. 'Ilary. Bitteres' day o' the year." He flung a handful of twigs at the fire. "Know what they are?" I shook my head again, conscious more than ever of my cockney ignorance. "Willer," he said, "willer, bellbine, elder an' rough scrub an' weeds. The no-good woods." He jabbed at the gutted hedge with his short-handled hook. "An' all outta thet. The thick bits I sell ter the 'urdlers, an' the thin bits I bundle inter faggits fer firin' an' pea-sticks. 'Edger's perks." He chuckled, and gave me the last square inch of his flattened roll. "Know 'ow ter lay an 'edge?" He forestalled the third miserable shake of my head with a cheerful one of his own. "No, 'course yer wouldn't. Look!"

The demonstration was suspiciously simple. He had already trimmed and left standing in the hedge a number of stout stems he called "stabbers" (he could, he said, have slashed them out and used split stakes instead, but these would have rotted where they entered the ground) and, between these, which were a yard or so apart, he now wove the thorn stools ("stowels", he called them), thick lengths of wood almost severed at the base and bent upwards to the top of the hedge. The bending encouraged the wood to form an abundance of shoots as well as checking the rising flow of sap. To complete the hedge and to make it impenetrable, he interlaced it with "binders", long slender hazel or wych elm rods. When he had finished he moved back to inspect it all. "There!" he said, "nobody couldn't deny as thet ent got no top nor bottom" which, as I had not yet come to grips with the Essex tongue, I thought better not to dispute.

I suppose relining a baker's oven was once regarded as a craft. The only baker in Moreton was Mr. Ball, and I cannot recall his oven being relined in my time. It had been in my Father's. When he told me about it my blood ran cold. Parts of the oven floor that had worn badly had to be hacked out and renewed. This could only be done between baking hours and at week-ends, and then only for a few minutes at a time because of the intense heat. The work was gruelling and exhausting. The "brickie" (as Father called him) lay at full length on the still-hot floor, his head at the sealed end and his feet at the other. There was one candle for light. When, the session ended, the brickie dropped from the door to lean against the wall outside to suck in air for the next, he was more dead than alive. "I dunno what 'e got fer the job," Father said, "but whatever 'e got 'e deserved it."

Not everyone would have agreed that marling was a craft. It was, nevertheless, a thriving industry in those areas where the soil was a mixture of sand, chalk and clay. It used to be said that the only good muck was the muck on the farmer's boots. All the same, he found it necessary to supplement it with malt-dust, horn-shavings, hog's hair, potash and sugar-baker's scum. Marl was a valuable substitute; it bound the soil and strengthened the wheat. In the 1870's, however, with the coming of "artificials", its use was discontinued, and the small bands of marlers who had plied their trade from village to village and farm to farm, gradually disappeared. The small round ponds in many an Essex field are the scars they left behind them.

When, with Chaucer's "primerolles", I sang my way along North Lane to the mill, grandmother used to warn: "Careful o' them there wells; they're as plentiful as mushrooms". They were. There was one in a room at the farm, one in "Back Medder", where we drew our water from, one close to the cottage where Father was born at Padler's End, and one opposite the signpost that pointed, half-way between "Wood Farm" and the sandpits, to Bovinger. No one seemed to know how they had got there or who had sunk them. Yet the digging of a well must have been a public as well as a perilous undertaking. I remember reading about two men who, overcome by "sudden and deadly steames, sunk down and irrecoverably dyed." There was, too, the danger from underground springs which could break and flood to the surface without warning. Gilbert White, in his "Journal", tells of a well two hundred and fifty feet deep. "John Gillman," he says, "an Ideot, fell to the bottom of it twice in one morning." The fairies must have been present at his birth for, White continues, "John survived the strange accident many years."

There were the indoor crafts. Grandmother made the most exquisite lace, with threaded bone bobbins restless over tiny brass pins; and aunt Lil, who produced patchwork and quilting that snatched the breath and dazzled the eyes, once made and embroidered a smock so unbelievably lovely that it was put under glass and displayed for months in the village hall. It was Virginia Woolf who said: "The peasants are the great sanctuary of sanity, the country the stronghold of happiness. When they disappear there is no hope for the race." Not to worry, Miss Woolf! With patience and time the mulberry becomes a silken gown. Soon or late we shall get back to old wisdoms, old beliefs, old behaviours, with the horse we stabled all our yesterdays ago back on tomorrow's roads ...

CHAPTER FOURTEEN

Like most Essex villages Moreton had its superstitious beliefs. They were not tangible like, say, Oxfordshire's "Whispering Knights". These were stones which, when the world was hushed, re-entered life as a king and his men. Witches and warlocks could not be seen, any more than God could be seen, but that did not stop them from working their spells. You spat on the sole of your shoe if you saw a white horse, or on the ground if you met a cross-eyed woman; and you never ignored a ladybird. If you found one you placed it in the palm of your hand and said:

"Ladybird, ladybird, fly away home.
Your house is on fire, your children are gone,
Except the little one under a stone,
Ladybird, ladybird, fly away home."

We never had in Moreton the paving-stones we had in London. If we had, we boys would have shunned the lines and sought the safety of the blank spaces. Treading on the lines would have meant getting our sums wrong. If the offenders were girls they would grow up to marry a black man and have a black baby. Grandmother Matthews was no gawping village maid, but she would sooner have stepped over a besom than over a beetle; if the beetle had crawled over her shoe a close friend would soon be dead. I suppose it was natural for a daughter to follow where a mother had gone. When, at the end of World War I, I found it necessary to catch up with neglected "homework", Mother gave me a "Touch-wood" for the end of my watch-chain. It would, she argued, help me to pass my exams. I cannot imagine what she would have done if she had seen me drowning — left me, perhaps, in the fond belief that I might become one of the Seven Swimmers, that happy breed of men able to save the lives of others in the same perilous plight.

My Father was "tarred wi' the sem ol' brush", though to a lesser degree. He had never seen an ambulance but when, later in life on his milk-boy's round at Loughton, he did see one, he exploded: "Thet's bad luck! If I don't find a black dog I'm gooin' ter brek me leg." Just like that. As if, inside him, the lid of a lore-filled well he knew nothing about had lifted and arrowed into his head the stuff of a superstition he had been familiar with all his life. Many of these superstitions were unwittingly based on common sense, like the one about opening your windows during a thunderstorm. We used to do that when the bombs rained down. But what can you say about breaking a mirror, or seeing the moon through glass? What can you say about trapping a robin, when all you wanted was that wily old sparrow everlastingly pinching your peas?

I have told elsewhere of what happened on Mrs. Crabbe's birthday, when I carried a bunch of hawthorn into the house. But that, heinous as it was to Mrs Crabbe, was the comedy of superstition. There was the drama of superstition; life and death poised in the scales, with death the victor by a grain. There was nothing scurrilous enough she could say about magpies. Two were for mirth and four were for birth, it is true, but there was always that first one for sorrow. I think it was Peggotty who said in "David Copperfield", "People can't die along the coast except when the tide's pretty near out." Well, you could die any old time the magpie was about, especially if you did not make in the grass the proper sign with your shoe. What was that mumbo-jumbo?

"I cross one magpie,
And one magpie crosses me;
May the devil take the magpie,
And God take me."

Mrs Crabbe defended her beliefs with a vehemence matching her size; but there were times when aunt Lil, up the Chase, trembled on the edge of apology for hers as if, being a woman, she should have known better. It was on such occasions that she sought to justify her weakness by exposing the weakness of others. "Tek 'em as lives at Cog'shall." Coggleshall was on the Roman road to Colchester. Here there was the finest specimen in all Essex of a merchant's town house, "Paycocke's". It was to "Paycocke's" in the 16th century that Thomas Paycocke had taken his young bride, "attyred in a gowne of sheepe's russet and a kirtle of fine worsted". There was "summat wrong" with "Paycocke's", ghosts cavorting over the ceiling's carved beams and clinking their chains behind the linenfold panelling. There was something wrong with the people of Coggleshall, too; they were "not all there". The men had a band. When they were told how good it sounded from the village street they downed instruments and went outside to listen to it. Then there was that ladder. It had been too short, so they had sawn off a rung from the bottom and nailed it to the top. And

103

that wheel-barrow bitten by a mad dog ... They were taking no chances with that; the wheelbarrow had been locked away in a shed in case it gave them all "the rabies". I have heard these stories many times since, but then they flooded me with a childish awe only to be equalled when, many years later, I discovered the fairy-tales of the brothers Grimm. I wish I had known then what I know now — how one of the four windmills at Stock Harvard had been demolished because there was only enough wind for three. I wonder what aunt Lil would have said to that!

Even "Owd Grannie Smith", insensitive as she was to things she could not see or touch, invested her bees with bell, book and candle, chatting to them in fair weather and in foul, and listening to them humming on Christmas Eve the Jubilate Deo. Perhaps she could be forgiven. Bees were a part of her life. They were "worritin' critters" at times. When they swarmed she chased them with an aching heart and an old tin pan and a spoon. If they settled they would become the property of the owner of the place of settlement. Her retrieving gear, sheepskin gloves and straw skip, was always to hand in the "back place". She did not need a veil. None of her bees had ever stung her; none of them ever would. Father told me once of the second-hand barometer he had bought for her at one of the "fairings". She handed it back to him with tears in her eyes. "Tha's a rum'n boy," she said, "I don't set no store by they. Kip it fer when yer weds. God's put 'is 'and in the sky; I kin tell all the weather I wants from thet." I think her omniscience was bolstered by the bees. When they flew back to their hives on a sunny day it was going to rain (it did), and when they grew suddenly noisy high winds and thunder were coming (they came).

She loved most of the things that had breath, but could not "abide" bats, those devil's angels that flew in the dark

to bring you misfortune. Whenever she saw one she tried
to propitiate it by chanting:

"Little bat, little bat, fly away over my head,
And you shall have a crust of bread;
And when I brew and when I bake,
You shall have a piece of my wedding-cake."

Just as the days had their superstitions, so had the
Festivals. The first one that comes to mind is Easter.
Grandfather Pettit bolted and barred the forge and
unbolted and unbarred it on the Monday that followed
Good Friday. That way Good Friday was safe. It was
wrong to shoe horses then. Shoeing horses meant nails,
and nails meant Pontius Pilate and the crucifixion. It
meant, too, the vengeance of Old Skrat, blood dripping
from the shoes to the floor and, out in the garden, spitting
from an indignant sky to spot the washing.

None of my aunts would allow holly to be brought into
the house before Christmas Eve or to be taken down
before Twelfth Night. Then it had to be thrown on the
'muck'll" and left to wither. If it was burnt someone in the
family was going to meet with a sticky end. This rough
treatment was not always meted out to mistletoe. It was
still called by some "All Heal", and was sometimes left
hanging from one Christmas to another in the belief that
it would bring luck and good health. It was frowned upon
by the church. When, in the Christmas of 1913, my own
vicar found a sprig in the greenery under the pulpit, he
ordered it to be removed and burnt. In those days the
road to a Merry Christmas must have been a harrowing
one, like having to map-read in a fast-moving stream of
traffic to see if, at the next crossing, it was left or right.

But the road was breasted by men and women with
unflagging zest, just as another road was to be breasted

by their daughters: the road to New Year's Eve. Superstition was rife enough then. The girls gathered in a quiet room of a quiet house and stood upside-down drinking mugs in the fireplace. Then they walked backwards up the stairs. In the morning they returned and lifted the mugs. Under one, perhaps, would be a sliver of wood, which foretold that the girl whose mug it was would marry a carpenter. Under another would be a clod of earth, which meant that somewhere in the offing was a farmer. I do not know if the girls were simple enough to believe all this, but it gave them something to speculate about. Stability in a waste of shifting sands. There was birth, there was death. Between the two there was the long littleness of living, drowsy tinklings lulling the distant folds. The superstitions were harmless, anyway, and comforting. You could plump back against them like a feather pillow and doze in a sweet content. It was easier to believe than disbelieve. When you were too near a thing you could not properly see it. It was like history. You did not know it was history when you were making it, but when you grew old and read about it you knew that it must have been.

Whatever the evidence, black, white or grey, I refuse to believe that my parents were such numskulls as to think that misfortune, if it came at all, would come when the broadbeans were in flower; or that baking an oatmeal cake containing the victim's urine would cast out a witch's spell; or that bread from the Communion Table would allay a child's cough; or that filling the mouth with water and sitting in front of a fire till the water boiled would stop toothache. And yet ... Joseph of Arimathea was kept alive for twelve years by the Holy Grail and every year, on 5th January, his staff on Wearyall Hill breaks miraculously into bloom; and every morning and night of our lives the sun is pulled up, or pulled down, by someone with an alarm-clock that never goes wrong.

It was Hazlitt who said: "Happy those who live in the dream of their existence, and see all things in the light of their own minds; who walk by faith and hope; to whom the guiding star of their youth still shines from afar, and into whom the spirit of the world has not entered."

Perhaps, after all, that is the only philosophy.

CHAPTER FIFTEEN

The Christmas I remember best began with a three-mile walk from Moreton to Ongar. I was then "on loan" to aunt Daisy who, with uncle Fred, was still living opposite the school. Aunt Daisy shopped at the International Stores at the Marden Ash end of the High Street in Ongar, close to the church and the house where David Livingstone stayed before setting out for Darkest Africa. Every Christmas she exchanged the coupons she got throughout the year for her purchases of Mazawattee tea for things she could give as presents.

The yearly ritual was an important one, but not nearly as important as the Ritual of the Christmas Puddings. Aunt Daisy would round up as many nephews and nieces as she could and set them to work cutting up the candied peel, stoning the plums, topping the currants and — the most fiddling job of all — scalding and skinning the almonds. She did not bother about the mess, or by what divers means we achieved our uncertain ends, and only reached over the table to rap us with a spoon when, tiring of the sticky plums, we plopped them into the rapidly swelling mound of fruit without attending to their innards. When it was all over, we stirred the mixture one at a time, wished, and were given a bright new penny to spend on a "lucky-dip" at the Two Miss Prentices over the road.

In those days Christmas, apart from its religious significance, was a time for "togetherness", and the togetherness of my uncles and aunts was something to be marvelled at. With nephews and nieces thrown in there were more of us to the square inch in Moreton than blades of grass, but we squeezed into aunt Daisy's cottage with the agility and singlemindedness of the animals squeezing into the Ark. Sleeping, which should have presented the biggest problem, was no problem to aunt Daisy. The women occupied the beds, the men the chairs and the floors, and we children had the time of our lives stowing "heads and tails". It was all so uproarious and good-humoured; it was all so calm. Aunt Daisy, who should have been worried out of her wits at the prospect of a couple of days' slavery over a fire that could belch out smoke like a feverish steamboat when it was minded to, was the calmest of us all. She sent the men to Bovinger for the bell-ringing, the women to the shed at the bottom of the garden to prepare the vegetables, and the children to the river for the "tiddlers" she said we could not possibly catch "wi' a worm an' a silly ol' pin'. Then she shut herself in the kitchen to start a meal which, a few hours later, would have the uncles and aunts dozing on their feet.

The languor of that afternoon, "gold-tinted like the peach", was something we found it hard to come to terms with. Strait-jacketed in our "on'y-fer-Sundays-an'-don'-git-tearin'-the-arse-out-on-'em!" we spilt into the empty and holy afternoon to peek through the holes in the blacksmith's door, or jerk the lazy water from the pump standing like a skinny scarecrow in the "Nag's Head" yard. Once, pricked by the bright spur of danger, we twitted the magpie in its wicker cage on the wall of old

Miss Crumble's cottage — but only once. Miss Crumble lived behind lace curtains and an aspidistra and was a witch. She could fix you with an evil eye and turn you into a mouse or, just as easily, make your ears grow till they were the size of an elephant's. Grandmother told me that she had been "frustrated" as a girl and had never got over it.

She must have been a clever witch. She could cure the whooping-cough by holding a spider over a child's head and chanting:

"Spider, as you waste away,
Whooping-cough no longer stay."

We had heard it whispered that, somewhere in her garden, safe from prying eyes and itching fingers, there was a root called pennyroyal. When, at the darkest hour of the night, a woman came crying to her for help, she crept like a cat into the garden and nipped off a piece of the pennyroyal, which she gave to the woman. The pennyroyal had miraculous properties. When the husband was looking the other way the woman put it under a gooseberry-bush in her own garden. That way she was safe. She would not have any additional mouths to feed then. It was all very odd.

The afternoon's aimlessnes lasted till tea-time. Things were different then. The food and the china were cleared away and the giggles and screams that came from the kitchen were transferred to the parlour almost before you could blink. Later the men played banker and dominoes and the women drew chairs to the fire and nattered. One of the aunts, who was "expecting" (we did not know what), had brought her knitting, and her needles, click-click-clicking to the rise and fall of her honest bosoms, provided a Christmassy drape to the room as soothing as it was right. The presents still had to be distributed from the tree. Aunt Daisy was not only a good cook; she was a good strategist, too. She wanted things to "hot up" and everyone to be in the right mood. The tree would be stripped in her own good time. This came sooner than expected. Uncle Frank pushed back his chair and exclaimed, "My! this room's like an 'ottus. Let's 'ev some air." The lovely December night that breezed through the window was like a tonic. Aunt Maude left the room to "stretch her legs", and uncle Fred slid quietly away for a red dressing-gown and a red piratical hat and to tie a foot-long strip of cotton-wool under his chin. When he returned he said in a smudgy voice:

"In comes I, Father Christmas,
Welcome or welcome not,
I 'ope ol' Father Christmas
Will never be forgot."

We cheered and he bowed and poked uncertainly between the candles, the pink and white sugar mice and the coloured glass balls for the presents. What turned out to be mine he picked up from the table supporting the tree. I opened it in the one quiet corner of the room. It was one of the toys I had carried with aunt Daisy all the way from Ongar — a steam engine! I stroked the brass cylinder and the tall black chimney and thought I should die from the sheer delight of possession.

When the clamour of "oohs!" and "ahs!" had subsided aunt Maude who, by this time, had "stretched her legs", opened the piano and announced that whether we liked it or not she was going to sing. That started the ball rolling well and truly. Everyone wanted to sing, even Bob Britton, one of uncle Fred's men and the only "alien" in the party. Bob (who must have been "owd" before he was born) was short and fat, with a head as shiny as a peeled onion and china-blue eyes twinkling in a burnt face that made you feel hot to look at it. He propped himself against the piano like a pocket-battleship. "I on'y know one song," he confessed, "but it's a good 'un." The song was "The Mistletoe Bough", and when he reached the lines:

> "Oh! sad was her fate, in sporting jest
> She hid from her lord in the old oak chest;
> It closed with a spring, and her bridal bloom,
> Lay withering there in a living tomb,"

he almost brought the house down. He certainly brought himself down. Surprised at his reception and forgetful of his physical limitations, he bowed — and spread-eagled himself across the pianist. He was disentangled in the end and given a chair and a tot of rum in the corner where I still stood fondling my engine. "A good 'un," he repeated; "it must've bin ter git me like thet." He flashed me a wink from those china-blue eyes and raised his glass. "Skin off yer nose, boy!"

After that it was a "free-for-all". Uncle Walter, with a tankard of beer in one hand and a cigarette in the other, frothingly "obliged" with "To be a farmer's boy-oy-oy", and my Mother sang a song containing the only verse I remember:

> "You can't holler down our drainpipe,
> You can't climb our apple-tree;
> I don't want to play in your yard,
> If you won't be good to me."

Uncle Will went one better than that. "This'll bring tears

112

ter yer eyes." he said. "We 'ad it at the Band of 'Ope." He
drained his glass, settled it on the piano, and sang:

"Father, dear father, come home with me now,
The clock in the steeple strikes one;
You promised, dear father, that you would come
  home,
As soon as your day's work was done.
Our fire has gone out, our house is all dark,
And mother's been watching since tea,
With poor brother Benny so sick in her arms,
And no one to help her but me.
Come home, come home, oh father, dear father,
come home."

The women sniffled at that, and uncle Frank acidly
remarked that some people didn't know the difference
between a decent song and a pub-crawl. What they
wanted was a *good* song. What about "Maud"? He did
not wait for an answer, but inveigled Maud into the
garden with his next breath. It was a more difficult
manoeuvre than he could have foreseen. He slurred to the
end of the first line with a ferocity that rushed him to
disaster in the fifth. "And the woodbine spices are wafted
abroad" was too much for teeth which, even had they
been his own, would have needed a setting of cement to
withstand an assault as wordily buttressed as that. They
flew over the floor and landed at my cousin Freda's feet.
Poor uncle Frank! It was not his night, for tragedy struck
again. Just as he was calling to Maud that he was here at
the ga-ate alone, aunt Lil shushed him to silence with
"The waits!" Uncle Frank knew when enough was too
much. He shuddered like a sinking ship and sadly called it
a day.
  We huddled at the door till the singers had finished "O

Little Town of Bethlehem", when aunt Daisy asked them in for mince-pies and a glass of elderberry wine. Then someone said, "What about another carol?". Uncle Fred turned out the lamp, so that the room was lit only by the fire, the fiddler tucked his instrument under his chin and we all sang:

"It came upon the midnight clear,
That glorious song of old,
From angels bending near the earth
To touch their harps of gold."

We could hear each other breathing in a room that by now was as packed as a sardine-tin, but, oh, how we sang! Never since have I heard a carol so sweetly rendered or one that so closely wrapped me round. It came to an end all too soon and, when the singers had gone and the lamps had been relit, everything seemed so serenely still, as if someone, too shy to make himself known, had silently blessed us and as silently stolen away. Aunt Daisy dabbed her eyes and said it was far too late for little children to be up, Christmas or no Christmas, and shooed us all to bed.

I was too excited to sleep. I could see on the table beside me the shining cylinder of my steam-engine, and could hear again the carol that still, I knew, flowed out to every corner of that skimpy room below. One of its lines kept recurring: "Peace on the earth, good-will to men." I was old enough to remember the agonies of the Boer War. Why did peace and good-will come only at Christmas? Peace and good-will ... Peace and good-will ... I reached out and brought my engine into bed with me. Happiness was such a lovely thing.

CHAPTER SIXTEEN

The time came when my parents deemed it advisable for me to return with them to London. My health had improved beyond all expectation, and the problem of "further education" now lifted its ugly head. I did not want to go back — oh, God! I did not want to go back. I had long ago been "accepted" and belonged to Moreton as much as its oldest inhabitant. Grandmother was the only person to interpret my sobbings aright. She tucked me up in my own little bed in my own little room and promised, "fer ever an' ever, Amen!" that every one of my school holidays would be spent with her.

It was a sop, but it was not a big enough sop. What had my Father said?

> "Moreton is my dwelling-place,
> And Christ is my salvation."

Well, Moreton was not going to be my dwelling-place ever again. When tragedy strikes we say, "Why should it have happened to me?" not, "Thank God it has never happened to me before!" and no counsel, however potent and to the point, is likely to make us think otherwise. The only feeling I can match up to the one I experienced then was that one in 1918, when I was detailed off to report to the "Vindictive" for her raid on the Mole at Zeebrugge. "You're going on special leave," smirked the drafting officer, "— *very special* leave. Say good-bye to your sweethearts and wives, 'cos you won't see *them* again." I recall as if it were yesterday that long walk to Chatham station. The air was like an unstoppered bottle of a lovely woman's scent, and the sun was high and red. I remember that sun. I stared at it and said inside me, "Zeebrugge ... I might never see you again after that." I remember the people, the birds, the trees. I kept thinking: "I'd like to touch you; you're real and alive — but, in a week or two's time, I won't be. I shall be dead!" That contrast again! The scales: the one pan loaded with life, the other with the dust and ashes of unfulfilled dreams. Somewhere on the way home to Mother and Father I think I must have cried. I am not sure; I must have done.

Grandmother kept her word. For the next few years every golden hour of every golden summer was spent at the farm. Then came the War. I went back again three times, once while the flags were still flying for a victory that was never properly ours, to jilt the girl I loved, once to see at Padler's End my Father's birthplace and once when, following the publication of an article of mine in the "Essex Countryside", I received an invitation from the then owners of Scotts Farm to pay it a return visit. Between the first and the last of these return visits there was a gap of over half a century.

But first things first ...

My cousin Ivy was one of the two daughters of aunt Daisy and uncle Fred, and I fell in love with her without knowing the first thing about it; then, just as the seed you planted in the year dot comes up behind your back, the love ripened and came to fruition. Maybe it was because, having flirted with death, I now saw life and saw it whole.

116

We became engaged and I went back to being a sailor. It was in Copenhagen that it all started. A stiffish wind was coming off the sea and the dhobeying on the fo'c'sle was flapping like the wings of wounded gulls. There were no books on pornography then, and I was reading in the British Medical Journal an item headed: "The prohibited degrees of relationship in marriage." It interested me. "The Act of —" Then it alarmed me. Ivy and I were cousins, and it was widely believed then that if there had been anything untoward in either of the families marriage between cousins could be dangerous. I thought I was getting hot-and-bothered about nothing. But was I? There was a nigger-in-the-woodpile, that story about an aunt who drowned herself in the river at the bottom of the garden.

I have always been fool enough to immolate myself on other people's altars. I immolated myself again. I wrote to the British Medical Journal and sought its advice. No reply. I wrote to my vicar (later to become the Bishop of Bathurst, Australia). This time there was a reply. The letter is before me as I write.

> "My dear Charles,
>
> I'm glad you wrote. You have every reason for your fears. Marriage between first cousins is wrong. However painful it may be to you, you must terminate your engagement at the earliest possible moment. Your fiancée will understand. Marriage is for life. You would never forgive yourself if — to put it mildly — things went wrong.
>
> My love to you — and God bless!
>
> P.S. Ephesians, Chap. 6 Ver. 11"

I dug out my Bible from my hat-box and turned up

117

Ephesians, Chap. 6, Ver.11. It read: "Put on the whole armour of God, that ye may be able to stand against the wiles of the devil."

It was a tragedy for both Ivy and me. We had played together, worked together, grown together. We had fallen in love together. Now we had fallen out of love together. No, that is not true. She had not fallen out of love with me, nor I with her. But that aunt who, one empty morning long ago, had walked out of life into death ... What about her? She would have cast a grey shade that no compassionate sun could have erased in a million years. I could not excuse myself; I did not dare. Marriage between cousins would not have frightened Ivy, but how could I have told her that if ever we had a baby it might be born a mongol? So when, on my next leave, we met at the sandpits and I "terminated" our engagement, I kept quiet, lashed with the whip of a scarlet tongue and blue eyes wet with tears forbidden to flow. Presently Ivy left me. She went down the Ongar Hill, over the Quasimodo bridge, and then up the gentle slope whose summit breasted the doors of the forge where my mother was born. That — the death of a world — was nearly sixty years ago.

"Put on the whole armour of God" ... I had to do that, all right. Mother referred to the incident — once — to aunt Maude. I heard her say, as a sort of *coup de grâce,* "We give birth to them, don't we? — but we never know what they're going to be like when they grow up." I could have confronted them and told them the truth. But why the hell should I have done? Sir Galahad, that purest and noblest of Arthur's knights, was not the only one privileged to put his feet under the Round Table ...

CHAPTER SEVENTEEN

The best way to see an English spring is to motor from uttermost north to uttermost south, for then, mile after new-green mile, you will see the last of March's madcap days trembling like an untutored bride into April's ardent arms.

That was how I saw Moreton that third time. I walked from the station to the "Red Cow", where I dawdled over a pint of ale as heady as any champagne. I dreamed down Shelley Hill (where Mother had lost her first gold watch), wondered by "Wood Farm" (where another of my cousins lives), and so came at last to the sandpits and Ongar Hill. I looked over my Moreton as, once upon a time, Moses must have looked over his Promised Land. To the left of me, at the foot of the hill, was the road that led to Padler's End. This time I left it behind to cross the bridge. Halfway over the bridge I stopped. Down below in that chuckling stream was where my school-mates and I had "dog-paddled" and imprisoned unsuspecting eels with forked sticks cut from the hedge. I gulped something down, half-sob, half-sigh. It was not real; it was all a dream.

The gentle rise from the bridge takes you into Moreton past what used to be the policeman's house (now resited

119

in Church Road) and what used to be Jones's, the "general stores" to the corner where the smithy had been. (The blacksmith's muscular son, Harry, had for a long time been one of my shining knights; then when he married a girl I would have bartered my young life for I hated him.) The shop (now the Alliance Food Stores and Post Office) stands a little way back down the hill. One of my uncles, a ship-shape-and-Bristol-fashion man, said it reminded him of a midshipman's chest: everything on top and nothing handy. Suspended from the ceiling were mousetraps, rubber boots, whalebone corsets, balls of string, oil-cans, bladders of lard, sides of bacon and goodness knows what; while on the counter were chunks of cheese which the women knowingly conned, probed and tasted — and often never bought. What especially intrigued me were the mounds of butter which, when he had hoped that you and yours were all quite well, Mr Jones tunnelled into, smacked to shape on a marble slab and then embossed with the figure of a cow or a clump of clover that had never been green nor ever would be. Nothing was pre-packed then; if it had been it would have been pitched into the privy, where it properly belonged.

I had a long day ahead of me, so decided to make my way to "Brook Lodge" first. The chapel was now a wreck. Inside were the pots and paints of an artist and outside the nettles and unkept grass of the devil. I stepped over rubble and bricks and looked through the windows. Surely this could not have been that house of God wherein, all those years ago, we had worshipped; or where, when it was warm with the Holy Ghost and stuttering paraffin lamps, the preachers — farmers, most of them — clawed from the skies a friend you could go walking with over the coffee-coloured clods thrown up by the plough! But it was. Surely it could not have been the place where that "ammonia woman" had so wondrously entertained us! But it was.

That "ammonia woman" was reed-thin and tall and smelt of prayer-books and hassocks. She wore without shame her "Sunday-go-to-Chapel" frock, a frowsy entanglement of black bombasine and point lace that fizzed as it swept the floor, and a black "Merry Widow" hat forever fretting a freckled face. She was a good musician, with a good musician's feeling for effect. When she played "For those in peril —" you sensed the surge of the sea and the venomous spit of its spray. The harmonium often failed her. Over its tormented years it had lost a lot of its wind and the woman's knees capered up and down like a fiddler's elbow to keep it going. At the end of the service, when all was still, she spiked the Blessing with staccato "Amens!" and "Praise the Lords!". Aunt Maude called her the "Hallelujah Chorus".

"Brook Lodge" seemed not to have changed at all. Some sort of stone column had been erected in the yard and a length of trellis fastened to the wall above the parlour, but the stables and hoppet were just as I had known them. I singled out the exact spot where I had stood on an upturned "Day and Martin" blacking box to harness "Blossom" and fancied I could still hear aunt Daisy singing:

> "Jolly boating weather,
> And a hay harvest breeze,
> Blade on the feather,
> Shade off the trees."

I remember asking her once why it should have been that particular song. She giggled like a schoolgirl and said, "Why shouldn' it be? Eton wer' yer uncle Fred's ol' school, wernt it?"

She was a lot happier at "Brook Lodge" than she had

121

been in that poky little house fronting the school. Uncle Fred was doing well, and money was coming in. Now there was no necessity for her to sweat from ten till four picking beans or peas for a measly five bob a week. Sometimes — but not very often — she harked back to the old days. "Yer shoulda sin me," she said, "—a sunbonnet on me 'ead, clod-'oppers on me fit an' a bit of 'ol sackin' coverin' me backside."

I stayed at "Brook Lodge" long enough to wonder if I could get permission to push at the stable-doors. Behind them, I felt, in some dark corner that had not been disturbed for sixty years, I would find a bike, a bike with no brakes, no free-wheel and with pock-marked rubber tyres that jolted the guts out of you ... I was getting heartsick and decided — none too soon — to get back to Moreton for something to eat. At High Laver bridge I glanced over my shoulder. "Brook Lodge" ... The old "Pig and Whistle" ... Who, seeing me now, would have guessed that sometimes after Chapel I had sat there, a stick of rock in one hand and a tawny-coloured confection like a ship's biscuit in the other? I was afraid of the dark, but when we started for home, past "Beehive Cottage" and the "Lindens", with the white ghost of Moreton Mill behind us, I clutched at an uncle's hand and gloried in the stars overhead and the gravel underfoot. This, on half-a-bottle of ginger-beer, was Life, if you like!

The once higgledy-piggledy cottages that stretched from the school to the church have been replaced by mod-con houses "fell-in-line", it would seem, by a sergeant major with a Wellington to his right and a Marlborough to his left. Slap in the middle of them is the police station, haunted, I have no doubt, by the ghost of that "Bobby" who, in 1904, dispensed the law and grew cabbages with hearts as big as his own. (He was, by the way, the first

122

policeman in Essex to be armed.) At the other end of Church Road, beyond the telephone booth on the green and end on to the Corner Houses, there are bungalows for the aged. There have been other losses, other gains but, despite them all, Moreton has remained the same, warm, friendly, peaceful, its people having had the sense to marry past with present that the union might have life and have it more abundantly.

Over the road from the "White Hart" is where the Two Miss Prentices kept their sweetshop. Here for a farthing you could get a handful of tiger-nuts or brandyballs or, if you wanted to cut a dash with that blonde thing sitting next to you at school, a bag of "Cupid's Whispers". The heart at seven is an unknown quantity; and it was much less chancy to slide over the desk in bulk an assortment of "I love yous!" and "Will you be mines?" than to say the same things to someone who might easily have fetched you an unlooked-for back-hander.

Next to the sweetshop stood a shed where bar fences and wattle hurdles were made, by, I think, the two brothers of the Two Miss Prentices. The skill expended on these afforded us almost as much entertainment as the blacksmith and his forge. I could not describe in a month of Sundays the craftsmanship that went into the hurdles, but the fences were simpler creations of cleft ash, drilled, chiselled, mortised and assembled on a wood frame sunk into the earth. (Later in life I was to see these fences in Romford, when the cattle market was held there, but, alas! like so many other things of good report, they have long since vanished.)

The pump, which stood in the "Nag's Head" yard, is now secured to the school wall "In Loving Memory". It was the source of most of the bad language in the village, only working when you poured a bucket of water into it and pistoned it back all rust till, minutes later, the rust had cleared and the water gushed from the spout like the glittering laughter of the first young thing you had ever kissed. The school, however, stands where it did, though it now boasts a glass-fronted extension flanked by ranch-fencing, and a television aerial.

Churches remind me of that rhyme:

"Every time I see a church,
I pay a little visit,
So when at last I'm carried in,
The Lord won't say 'Who is it?' "

Notwithstanding, except for saluting grandmother Matthew's grave, I did not "pay a little visit" to St. Mary's. I was anxious to get to Scotts Farm. I walked expectantly up Maltings Hill, savouring to the full the flavours to come. On the right of me was the field where aunt Maude had been tossed by a bull and, on the left of me, a string of Council houses. Then, round the corner by North Lane — Scotts Farm! — patient, untroubled, with not one grey hair in its head. "It's waiting for me!" I mumbled, and the tears rolled down my cheeks. I was not ashamed of them. Scotts Farm had been the bottom rung of my ladder back to health. Until then I had seen the country only through the eyes of my parents and my coloured picture books. It was a world with real cows, real sheep, and hedges so green with the thrust of spring that for days I was afraid to go near them, lest a still small voice behind me should say, "Don't you dare! for the place whereon thou standest is holy ground."

CHAPTER EIGHTEEN

Scotts Farm is now in the possession of Mr Kenneth Bird, his attractive wife, Margaret, and their three children. "We've been here eight years," Kenneth told me, "and have loved every minute." And why not? The air is sweet and clean, the villagers are good neighbours, and the rich brown earth is second to none. It was John Norden who in Tudor times wrote: "This shire is moste fatt, frutefull, and full of profitable thinges, exceeding anie other shire for the general comodeties and the plentie, so that it seemeth to me to deserve the title of the English Goshen, the fattest of the Lande; comparable to Palestina, that flowed with milke and hunnye."

The exterior of Scotts Farm has altered little. In the yards some of the sheds have been pulled down, but the functional ones remain. The plough which, when it was not "opening a top" or furrowing "reg'lar like", had lain on its side near the pond, had long since been disposed of. It had been a good and faithful servant, just as the farmer's wife before it had been a good and faithful servant. A porch has been added to the front of the house and a conservatory to the wall facing the Moreton-Fyfield road. The conservatory is a boon and a blessing. It tempers the north wind and provides warmth for the grapes, melons and tomatoes. It also makes an ideal setting for the consumption of Margaret Bird's butter, cream, scones and jam. The butter, the rich gold of peggles, raced me back to grandmother. She, too, had made butter: overnight cream from the milk rotated by hand for an hour in a wooden tub to the accompaniment of a piece of doggerel as ancient as the hills. But no wooden tub for Margaret. "Five minutes under the electric mixer and Bob's your uncle!"

The rooms were as I remembered them in those "sweet childish days that were as long as twenty days are now", with stairs leading up and stairs leading down. Here a door had been sealed off and there an opening had been formed for a window. In what had been my own room, where an alien bed now twitted my prentice years, I looked down and out into the yard. There, on that very patch of grass, grandmother had nudged me to school with what she called "me 'ol Gallic blessin' "

"May the roads rise with you;
May the winds be always at your back;
And may the Lord hold you in the hollow
of His hands."

Downstairs was the "well-room", where the gritty voice of a man they called Caruso had come from a box which, with a black cylinder and a shiny brass horn decorated with a listening dog, one of my aunts said was a "grannyphone".

I passed from room to room in a daze. There was a toilet "down" and a bathroom "up". I turned a tap with an unbelief as real as the tap itself. There was no water here; there could not be. Water had to be fetched from the well in the field beyond the stables in buckets slung from a yoke. But water *was* here, a glistening gush that half-

126

twisted me to the door to hear — as for one crazy moment I thought I might — grandmother's: "Goo easy wi' the water, boy; it don't grow on trees, yer know." And the bath ... That was long, narrow-waisted, and as shiny as wet snow under the moon. Somehow it did not "belong". The only bath I had known had been a round one. You squatted in this, your chin on your knees, listening to the bubble of splashed water against the fire's hot bars, and praying at the same time that the good Lord would let you climb out of the thing without upsetting it and yelling your head off for help.

There were other things that did not belong: the washing machine, the deep-freeze, the central heating, the infra-red grill. Yet each was right and proper. The house that stands still is the house that dies. "And," Margaret Bird confessed, "ours nearly did die. We knew how we wanted it to look, but somehow we couldn't get it that way. People who thought us mad didn't help. Kenneth had read Law at Cambridge, and I'd taken History at Reading. What could youngsters like us want with a place like this? They didn't know the answers, but we did, and most of them were the right ones." She pointed to the children playing where the "none-so-pretty" still groped for the late sky. "One day, when the world is no longer their oyster, we want them to come back to where they knew their greatest happiness." She smiled. "You've done it yourself, you know.

'God gave all men all earth to love.
But since our hearts are small,
Ordained for each one spot should prove
Beloved over all.' "

"Ah!" I said, "Kipling".
"And Burwash."

127

"No — and Moreton."

She smiled again. 'You never know. Perhaps in one of those 'Jungle Books' the right words lost the way. Let's blaze a trail. It *was* written of Moreton."

"And Scotts Farm."

She laughed this time. "There's no holding you, is there? I'm going to agree. Motion carried *nem. con.* Shake!"

We shook.

Kenneth Bird does not farm his five acres. 'I milk the cow in the morning," he said, "and round up the livestock — the donkey, the dog, the ducks, the goose, the cats and the bull-calf. That's about all. Then I hare off to the office at Harlow. Both of us work on the farm till its dark, and at week-ends we go flat out. But it's our life, and we love it." He stabbed a finger towards the fields and the few coloured inches of "Wood Farm" lifting above the trees. "Look at all that. Beauty that nearly chokes you." He turned suddenly, flinging over his shoulder: " 'He findeth God who finds the earth He made.' Come and see the barn."

The barn was — as it always had been — a vast pile of oak and soft distances lazing out from a primal past to meet on the rim of the world the shape of things to come. It made my heart ache. In it, down unremembered years, the Mummers had mimed and St. George had slain with "trusty sword and true" a long succession of Bestial Beelzebubs. In it, too, when the last sheaf from the last field had been carted and the "corn baby" pulled to the top of its pole, the labourers had sat down to a "mel supper", paid for from the "largess" monies donated by the farmer and his friends.

"We have ploughed and we have sowed,
We have reaped and we have mowed,

128

We have brought home every load.
Hip, hip, hip, the Harvest Home!"

Kenneth Bird pricked the Past. "I like coming in here," he whispered; "there's always someone I feel I ought to shake hands with."

****

In a book such as this it would be wrong for a biased author to have the last word. I therefore quote with gratitude from Joan Forman's "Haunted East Anglia" :

"Throughout its history Essex has retained one rich constant — agriculture and the manners and customs of that way of life. There is still something slow, steady, unshakeable in the country people. Their memories are long, their histories fruitful, their wisdom deep, To talk to them is to go back in time to an older, pleasanter and happier England."

- - - - oOo - - - -